SOLANYELY RUIZ

DARIEN

The Shadow Behind the American Dream

O!
Ediciones

Darién: The Shadow Behind the American Dream

© Solanyely Ruiz

First Edition
September 2024

Edited by:
O! Ediciones
www.oediciones.com
RRSS: @oediciones

Legal Deposit No.: DC2024001578
ISBN: 978-980-452-008-2

Author:
Solányely Ruiz
hortearo@oediciones.com

RRSS:

Editor:
Orlando DJ Hernández
editor@oediciones.com

Cover Design:
Marianyely Ruiz
marianyelyruiz@hotmail.com

Darién

Where fear and faith collide with migrants who are betting on a better future.

Dedication

This publication is dedicated to all those who, with unwavering courage, have crossed the Darién Jungle in search of the American dream. To those who, guided by a primal instinct, dare to venture into the unknown, facing challenges with determination and bravery.

To those who have found support in strangers who become their companions along the way, sharing laughter, tears, and hopes during the journey toward a better future. To those who, driven by a dream, endure thirst, hunger, and overcome their deepest fears.

Every page of this publication serves as a reminder of the inner strength and human ability to achieve the unattainable. May their stories inspire others to pursue their own dreams with courage and determination.

With deep respect and admiration.

Acknowledgments

*First, I thank God for giving me
a life filled with joy and grace.*

*To my husband, Jesús Eduardo Rodríguez,
I am deeply grateful.
His unique way of being inspires me to keep
moving forward and to fulfill each of my dreams.*

*To all the people who have trusted me
to share their stories,
I am immensely thankful.
Their tales have made my heart
grow and have made me a better person.*

Solanyely Ruiz

Allow me to introduce myself: I am Solanyely Ruiz, a migrant and Venezuelan lawyer, with a deep passion for justice and solidarity. My journey in the legal world began in 2009, after studying Accounting. It was during that time, as I became familiar with the laws involved in my education, that I felt inspired to specialize in Venezuelan Law, driven by the dream of defending the most vulnerable and seeking justice for those without a voice. Over time, I discovered that my calling extended beyond individual defense and the borders of a single country. I have developed the ability to understand the legal system of any nation with a simple reading, which has allowed me to promote respect from both a legal and human perspective.

I am a joyful person, always looking to bring smiles where they are most needed. In 2018, I made the brave decision to leave my beloved Venezuela in search of a more promising future. With a visa that took me to Chile, I lived three years of deep learning, experiencing what it means to be new in a country different from the one where I was born. Chile became my home, a wonderful country where people always made me feel welcome. Emigrating brings countless experiences, so many that telling them all would require another book.

In 2021, I followed my heart and ventured to the United States with my life partner. Arriving in the land of dreams and opportunities was a challenge: I didn't understand the system, I didn't speak the language, and those around me hadn't yet found a clear path to help me. Amid the uncertainty of how to legalize my status in the U.S., I discovered my true passion: immigration processes. Finding my own way made me realize how difficult it is to navigate this system, and that revelation sparked in me the desire to help others. Since then, I've committed to being a bridge, easing the processes so that other migrants can start their new lives without stumbling in the darkness of the unknown.

Today, I can affirm that behind every migrant, there is a real and emotional motive, accompanied by profound experiences. Leaving one's homeland involves much more than a geographical change. However, those of us who choose the United States share a common goal: to live the American dream.

Since I began supporting other migrants, I've had the privilege of hearing countless stories of resilience and hope. Each of these stories reinforces the importance of our shared humanity and the power of community to build a more just and compassionate world for all.

With this work, I want to offer a window into the experiences and challenges of those who dare to pursue their dreams, often facing traumatic situations. What is happening with migrants at this moment deserves our attention.

This book is dedicated to all those who have entrusted me with their deepest secrets about their journeys, and it seeks to shed light on the unimaginable: the existential crises experienced while crossing the most natural passage of the Americas, the Darién. Nearly 500,000 people have crossed the Darién jungle in 2023, according to a report by Doctors Without Borders (MSF). However, here, I will share only a few of those stories.

This book is for those who are now part of the United States, contributing to the development of this great nation with their work, experiences, and contributions. To all those who, through hard work, have learned to regularize their status and comply with every established rule, so that their children can be the true protagonists of the American dream, even though at some point they faced situations that made them feel they could not go on.

As a legal specialist, I advocate for the adherence to the laws of every country, especially in the United States, where I currently reside. But, as a human being, I know we can be better; I know we can change many things for the greater good.

It is time to become aware: human suffering is sometimes not defended by any law, but our humanity has the responsibility to balance these situations.

Content

Introduction

We will embark on a journey that will challenge our hearts and lead us to explore the depths of the human soul. We will delve into a realm of diverse experiences, where hope intertwines with pain, despair meets resilience, and dreams confront the harsh reality of existence.

In the following pages, you will discover the story of those who have defied the shadows of oblivion, who have crossed the boundaries of fear and uncertainty in search of a better life. It is the story of Venezuelan migrants who have faced the greatest challenge of their lives: crossing the infamous Darién on their path toward the "American Dream."

But beyond being a mere travel chronicle, this is a narrative of humanity in its purest form. It is a story of courage in the face of adversity, of solidarity among strangers, and of hope in the darkness. It is a call to action, an invitation to open our eyes and hearts to the realities around us and to recognize our shared responsibility toward our brothers and sisters in the world.

In our daily lives, we often distance ourselves from the complexities of extreme human experiences, without considering that we ourselves might not be able to face similar situations. However, this is an opportunity to immerse yourself in the true feelings of a migrant on foot, someone who, unlike us, had to keep going even when their body screamed that it could no longer continue.

So, dear reader, prepare yourself to dive into an ocean of emotions and raw truths. In these pages, you will find stories not only of pain and loss but also of love and redemption. I challenge you to find the light amid the shadows, hope amid the chaos, and truth amid the confusion.**

This is your journey, your search for meaning and purpose in a world often torn apart by suffering and injustice. Take my hand, dear reader, and together we will explore the depths of the human soul and rise toward the light that awaits us at the end of the tunnel.

Let us observe together how the barriers created by man are not capable of breaking the true dreams that drive both body and soul toward the unknown, in a world where motivations are shaped by social media. Every day, we see how anyone can desire what another person has simply because a social network opened the door to that desire.

We will uncover the motivations behind the chaos at the U.S. border and how each step taken by those walking is filled with relentless determination to overcome obstacles, turning their journey into a true struggle for survival and hope.

Chapter 1
Human Migration

Migration has been a constant throughout human history, shaping civilizations, economies, and cultures. Driven by the pursuit of better living conditions, resources, and the need to escape conflicts, it has left an indelible mark on our species. From the nomadic tribes of antiquity to the transoceanic migrations of the modern era, each movement has influenced the course of nations.

The reasons behind migration are as diverse as societies themselves. The search for resources, such as water and fertile land, has been a primary driver since the dawn of civilization. In the modern era, economic and educational opportunities have become the main factors attracting people to more prosperous regions, where prestigious universities and dynamic labor markets act as magnets for those seeking a better future.

Additionally, migration forced by armed conflicts, persecution, and natural disasters remains a reality. In the 21st century, climate change has added a new dimension to migration, creating so-called "climate refugees," who face the daunting task of adapting to a world in constant environmental flux. This scenario highlights the interconnectedness of environmental issues and human rights.

The effects of migration are profound in both sending and receiving regions. In areas of origin, migration can relieve demographic pressure and reduce unemployment, but it can also lead to a brain drain, weakening the productive and innovative capacity of countries. This loss of talent can have devastating long-term consequences.

On the other hand, in receiving countries, migration can drive economic growth and enrich cultural diversity. However, it can also generate social and political tensions. Inadequate integration of migrants can exacerbate issues such as xenophobia and competition for resources, underscoring the need for inclusive policies that celebrate diversity as a strength.

Today, migration is more complex than ever. Globalization and information technologies have facilitated mobility, but restrictive policies and strengthened borders have created an increasingly hostile environment, especially for those seeking asylum. The images of fortified borders and anti-immigrant rhetoric reflect a world where human mobility faces growing obstacles.

This phenomenon also raises ethical and human rights questions. Protecting the rights of migrants and refugees, along with their effective integration, is essential for modern societies. International cooperation is crucial to addressing the challenges and seizing the opportunities presented by migration. Only through a comprehensive and humanitarian approach can this phenomenon be adequately managed, ensuring the well-being of all involved and promoting a more dynamic and culturally rich society.

Since the beginning of my life as an immigrant, I encountered a striking reality: the lack of knowledge and understanding about migration processes among migrants themselves and the difficulty in asserting their human rights. It's astonishing to see that, beyond the agencies that regulate migration in each country, there is no governmental entity dedicated to facilitating the integration of immigrants. In other words, there is an entity that legally regulates migration, but there is no organization to help decode the complex puzzle of settling into a new country.

People who are far from knowing a clear path to success often follow the steps of others, who are frequently misguided. In interacting with people who have decided to take on the difficult journey of migration, I noticed that many lack basic information on how to navigate this intricate labyrinth of laws and regulations.

Uncertainty and fear define their lives, not for lack of willingness to follow the rules, but because they don't know what those rules are. The immigrant wavers between the desire to do things right and the condemnation of not knowing what the right path is.

Many animals migrate each year in search of the best places to give life to their offspring, which is completely logical: to choose the best environment for their children to thrive. However, human migration is entirely regulated. You cannot move freely across the world without encountering barriers, often taller than the walls themselves.

From a spiritual perspective, migration transcends physical borders and explores the boundaries of our deepest dreams and aspirations. We move because it is part of our nature, but our minds do not recognize laws or obstacles; these are human creations designed to limit our actions. The desire to move, to explore the unknown and seek new horizons, is ingrained in our being. Migration is a manifestation of our ability to dream and to always seek beyond the known.

Since time immemorial, migration has been an intrinsic part of the human experience. Whether out of necessity, the search for opportunities, or simply the longing for change, we have embarked on journeys that transcend the material, seeking belonging and fulfillment beyond geographic coordinates. The stories of migrations and conquests run through our veins, to the point where we often don't really know where we belong. This blend of stories and destinies defines us, and in every migrant lives the legacy of countless generations who also sought a better place to live.

At the heart of every migrant lies a dream, a longing to reach a destination that resonates with their innermost being. These dreams act as beacons in the darkness, guiding us through the uncertainty and challenges along the way. The goal gives meaning to the journey, even if we don't know how the path will unfold. It is the dreams that give us courage in moments of doubt, fueling hope even when difficulties seem insurmountable. We are driven by the mission to arrive where we wish to be, with an inner strength that pushes us forward despite obstacles and adversities.

Migration, from a spiritual perspective, is also a journey of self-discovery and transformation. Stepping out of our comfort zone forces us to adapt and redefine ourselves in our new environment. What is useful to us, we keep; what we don't need, we leave behind. In this way, we transform into new people.

Migration is a process of shedding the superficial layers of identity to connect with the purest essence of our being. On this journey, we encounter ourselves more deeply, facing fears, overcoming limitations, and discovering the inner strength that resides within each of us. We learn to do things we never would have experienced in our home country, and the need to survive allows us to value our true potential much more.

Journeys like the Camino de Santiago, traveled each year by thousands of people known as pilgrims, remind us that migration is not just a material matter, but also a spiritual quest.

As we cross physical borders, we also traverse emotional and spiritual borders, weaving a network of connections that transcend distance and time. On our journey, we find soul companions, people whose destinies intertwine with ours in inexplicable ways. These connections, based on empathy and solidarity, are a testament to the transformative power of migration, which unites people from different cultures and backgrounds into a shared fabric of humanity. Through simple gestures, fatigue, hunger, and thirst are expressed in a universal language that reinforces our shared humanity, creating a global community where each individual has a place and a purpose.

Beyond the family and friends who await us, migration is the unshakable belief in a better future, the certainty that by changing our location, we will have the opportunity to build a more fulfilling life. Migrants chart a path toward an unknown destination, trusting in a greater force that guides them. This drive is not merely material; it is an expression of the human spirit seeking fulfillment, dignity, and belonging in a world that often seems indifferent to their hopes.

During migration, people transcend the limitations of the body and mind, embracing their spiritual being. Each step is an opportunity to grow, learn, and find their place in the vast universe that surrounds them. Despite legal restrictions, the American dream continues to be pursued by human beings against all odds. Resilience and hope are the true compasses that guide migrants through unknown landscapes and unforeseen challenges, toward a horizon full of promise.

My experience with each migrant has made me understand the critical importance of education and awareness in the realm of migration and human rights. I have committed my professional life to filling this gap in knowledge, providing support and guidance to those who bravely and determinedly face the challenges of migration. Through my work, I strive to empower people, equipping them with the necessary tools to safely and legally navigate their pursuit of a better life. Each step we take together inspires me.

§

Chapter 2
The Exodus Through the Darién

Addressing the topic of the South American exodus through the Darién is to venture into a territory where bravery and survival reach their most extreme limits. This journey not only showcases sheer physical endurance but also compassion, solidarity, and, often, despair. The stories that emerge from this passage are not merely accounts of travel, but modern epics of resilience, where every step can mean the difference between life and death.

The magnitude of the migratory phenomenon through the Darién is understood by few. While more than half a million people have crossed this jungle, millions more remain unaware of the severity of this humanitarian crisis. These migrants are not just statistics, but individuals whose stories challenge simplistic notions of what it means to be a refugee or an immigrant seeking a better life.

Attempting to legislate the humanitarian reasons driving this exodus is a task riddled with contradictions and moral dilemmas. Laws, often written in broad terms, are applied unevenly based on the discretion of those who enforce them. This can result in decisions that, far from being just or humane, become harsh and inhumane, stripping migrants of their dignity.

In the past three years, migration to the United States has reached unprecedented, massive levels. There is a widespread misconception of open borders and near-guaranteed legal access, where the language barrier often leads to misinterpretations of U.S. law. This false promise has led many to believe that the barriers that once prevented them from achieving the American dream have disappeared. What were once clearly defined limits are now seen as surmountable obstacles, driven by the belief that success and prosperity are within reach for all, if only they dare to try.

Digital marketing and the idealization of life in the United States have played a crucial role in fueling this narrative. From a young age, Latin Americans have been bombarded with images of wealth, success, and happiness through movies, TV shows, and, more recently, social media. These stories have created an obsession with the American lifestyle, leading many to risk everything in search of that promised paradise.

On their journey toward this dream, migrants move forward step by step, without a clear direction, driven by a survival instinct that pulls them back to their most primitive roots. Under the scorching sun and the ominous shadows of the jungle, they fight not only against the elements but also against their own fears and weaknesses. Their bodies, exhausted and battered, keep pushing forward, guided by the hope of a better future for themselves and their families.

Migrants dare to reveal their most primal instinct, motivated by the testimonies of those who have managed to cross the imposing jungle. What these walkers face in the Darién is not so different from what explorers of the past experienced during the conquests, when they ventured into unknown territories in search of riches and glory.

At that time, the conquerors faced the unknown with the intention of exploring and discovering new lands rich in resources. Their motivation was primarily economic, driven by curiosity about what the planet could offer them. However, what is happening now in the Darién is a consequence of classism and inequality that have left many behind in a world that is advancing rapidly. In an era of technology and progress, many are forgotten, relegated to the margins of society. This large group of people, educated and familiar with land, water, or air transportation technologies, chooses this route as a means of escape to bypass the migration controls imposed in Central America. The motivation is clear: no one can stop them from walking, especially in an unregulated and unwatched place.

Every person who decides to cross this jungle does so driven by a reason that surpasses fear. For them, the Darién is just one more step in a much larger process. Since 2020, more than half a million people have crossed this jungle, increasingly prepared and less afraid. These travelers have developed remarkable resilience, facing the hell of the Darién with a determination that defies all logic. Meanwhile, governments are desperately seeking ways to curb these dreams that seem unstoppable.

Behind each of these travelers is a story marked by struggle, sacrifice, and, in many cases, tragedy. More than half a million unique accounts describe this passage as a journey of death or terror. Many underestimated the difficulty of each kilometer, believing it would be easier than it truly is. Among the migrants are professionals, workers, wrongdoers, and people of all kinds. Generalizations cannot be made; human diversity is reflected in each of them, showing how human beings, regardless of their origin or condition, are willing to take risks that defy all reason.

Some flee from political repression, persecution, and discrimination in their home countries. For them, returning is not an option; it is a death sentence. They prefer to face the unknown and the dangers of the Darién, where death is a constant possibility, rather than resign themselves to a fate marked by oppression. Listening to their stories, laden with fear and hope, inevitably inspires deep admiration for their courage. Each step they take is a declaration of their right to live in freedom.

Others do not flee from immediate danger but find danger in the majestic jungle. There are those seeking to reunite with loved ones, lovers separated by cruel circumstances, dreaming of feeling the warmth of an embrace again. I have heard stories of couples who, after years of separation, risk everything for that reunion. And then there are those who, tired of the borders that confine them, in an act of rebellion and hope, venture onto this illegal path, determined to survive any obstacle.

This exodus through the Darién is a testament to human resilience, to the ability of people to defy the impossible in search of a better life. It is a reflection of internal and external struggles, of despair and hope, of courage and fear. It is a story of human beings who, despite the circumstances, refuse to give up and continue moving forward, one step at a time, toward an uncertain future, but one full of possibilities.

The Venezuelan Exodus

The crisis in Venezuela has reached devastating proportions in recent years, becoming one of the worst humanitarian crises in recent Latin American history. This disaster is not the result of a single factor, but rather a combination of political, economic, and social circumstances that have plunged the country into unprecedented chaos and despair. The Venezuelan exodus is a reflection of the struggle for survival and dignity in the face of systemic collapse.

On the political front, Venezuela has endured more than two decades under an authoritarian regime, first led by Hugo Chávez and later by his successor, Nicolás Maduro. During this period, democratic institutions have been systematically dismantled, freedom of expression severely restricted, and political persecution has created an atmosphere of repression and unprecedented polarization. This process has fostered a climate of fear and powerlessness, forcing many Venezuelans to flee in search of freedom.

A sense of powerlessness can be felt in every corner of the country. In every conversation, in every fearful whisper, the shadow of a regime that controls the future of its citizens with an iron fist looms. This repression is not only physical but also psychological, weakening hope and fueling the desire to escape to a place where life can be lived freely.

In 2024, Venezuelans face the greatest challenge in our history: making the world understand that the decision of more than seven million people to leave the country is directly related to the imposition of Nicolás Maduro, despite the democratic will to peacefully remove him from power.

The economic crisis in Venezuela has been equally devastating. The country has experienced runaway inflation, a free-falling currency, chronic shortages of food and medicine, and an economic collapse that has left the nation in ruins. But what Venezuelans fear most is persecution; unable to express their discontent without risking unjust imprisonment, they feel increasingly suffocated by the regulation of social media, which further limits freedom of expression.

Venezuela today is like a child receiving brutal blows from its father but unable to cry; it must endure each strike in silence, fearing that the next beating will be worse. The rich grow richer, while the poor sink deeper into poverty. And amid it all, professionals—those who once dreamed of prosperity—are condemned to live in poverty.

This collapse is not just a set of statistics; it is a reality lived by millions of people who struggle daily to access even the most basic necessities. Corruption and mismanagement have left the country stripped of resources, creating an environment where desperation is the norm. Friends and family are forced to make unimaginable sacrifices, selling what little they have and abandoning their dreams just to survive one more day.

In this context, many Venezuelans seek refuge in countries that the Chavista regime has demonized for decades. The official narrative has painted the United States as the great enemy, responsible for all of Venezuela's ills. Yet, it is precisely there that many Venezuelans seek a new beginning. This fact demonstrates the power of desperation and the need for survival, which surpasses any political ideology.

Venezuela is a country of extreme contrasts. While some live in ostentatious luxury, others are trapped in such deep poverty that it is difficult to imagine. Wage earners make less than 20 dollars a month, an amount insufficient to cover even the most basic needs. This chasm between the rich and the poor has widened into an insurmountable gap, separating Venezuelans into two entirely different realities.

I have seen friends, people who once had prosperous careers and ambitious dreams, relegated to selling anything they can on the streets, simply to bring some food to the table. This phenomenon is not just economic, but deeply psychological, marking those who have been stripped of their dignity and forced to fight for survival in an increasingly hostile environment.

The crisis in Venezuela has affected not only the economy and politics but also the social fabric. Violence and crime have reached alarming levels, making the country one of the most dangerous in the world. However, in recent times, crime has decreased, as even criminals have fled the crisis, and in many cases, end up engaging in criminal activities in other countries, which does not represent the true values of Venezuelans.

The lack of access to basic services such as healthcare and education has exacerbated the humanitarian crisis. Millions of Venezuelans struggle to survive in conditions of extreme hardship. Many people die from treatable diseases because they cannot find treatment or simply cannot afford it. The government, in its effort to maintain control, shirks all responsibility: it does not answer for healthcare, the economy, or the well-being of its citizens. It is just a small circle of power, fewer than 500 people, deciding the fate of more than 25 million Venezuelans who still remain in the country.

Each day is a battle for survival, a struggle against a system determined to crush any glimmer of hope. While the shortages of food and medicine are not as severe as in previous years, the high cost of living and the lack of decent wages remain constant threats to the stability of the average Venezuelan.

These factors have triggered a massive exodus of Venezuelans fleeing in search of safety, stability, and opportunities abroad. It is estimated that more than seven million Venezuelans have left their country in recent years, making this migration crisis one of the largest in the world, despite the fact that the country is not at war. This exodus is a physical manifestation of Venezuela's collapse, a reflection of desperation and the search for a future that, for many, is no longer possible in their homeland.

Despite the magnitude of this crisis, the regime continues to propagate the narrative that those who leave are wrong, traitors. I have heard the voices of those who stay, their reasons and fears, and I have seen the pain in the eyes of those who depart, leaving behind not just a country, but also a life and an identity.

Even in the midst of one of the worst humanitarian crises in recent history, Venezuelans have shown an extraordinary capacity for resilience. The fighting spirit and the ability to find joy, even in the midst of extreme adversity, are characteristics that define our people. Although the crisis has plunged millions into poverty and suffering, many Venezuelans maintain a positive and optimistic outlook on life, facing challenges with determination and good humor.

Humor, in particular, has been a vital tool of resistance. In the darkest moments, the wit and creativity of Venezuelans are reflected in jokes, memes, and humor that, though sometimes dark, offer relief in the midst of hardship. This sense of humor serves as a pressure valve, a way to maintain sanity and hope when everything else seems lost.

Beyond humor, the sense of brotherhood and solidarity has been a cornerstone throughout this crisis. The Venezuelan community, both inside and outside the country, has come together to support one another in times of need. This solidarity is evident in small acts of generosity, in the emotional support shared among friends and family, and in the collective effort to confront the challenges that life imposes.

As Venezuelans seek refuge in other countries, we face new challenges in the form of discrimination and xenophobia. Although Venezuela has a long history of welcoming migrants from various parts of the world, we now find ourselves confronting exclusion in the countries where we seek safety.

The increase in visa requirements and the migration restrictions imposed by some Latin American countries have made our path to security and stability even more difficult. These policies, designed to control migratory flows and protect the socioeconomic stability of receiving countries, have created additional barriers, forcing us to resort to more dangerous and clandestine routes. This has increased the risk of exploitation, human trafficking, and other abuses during our journey toward a better future.

Rejection and barriers are not only political but also social. Negative stereotypes and prejudices against Venezuelan migrants have contributed to our social exclusion, making it more difficult to integrate into new communities. This rejection not only impacts our opportunities for employment and education but also erodes our dignity and sense of belonging.

It is crucial to address these issues with seriousness and empathy to fully understand the impact of the Venezuelan migration crisis and work toward solutions that promote solidarity, inclusion, and respect for the human rights of all migrants. International collaboration and regional cooperation are essential to tackling the complex challenges associated with our migration and ensuring an effective and just humanitarian response.

Our journey, marked by the hope for a better future, is also a constant struggle against adversity and prejudice. Every step we take is a testament to our strength and determination and a call for empathy and action to build a world where everyone can live with dignity and respect. Despite the challenges, we press on with the firm conviction that a better future is possible—not just for us, but for all who dream of a place where they can live in peace and freedom.

We may be far from Venezuela, but our hearts remain there, still dreaming of freedom. This 2024 has been a year of connection for us: our baseball team won the Caribbean Series, our soccer team played like never before, and our Venezuelan brothers and sisters raised their voices with a "¡Fuera Maduro!" so loud that it resonates in every corner of the world.

§

Chapter 3
Ana

Ana made the hardest decision of her life at 33 weeks pregnant: to embark on a dangerous journey with the sole goal of giving birth to her child in a place where he could grow up in peace and safety. Her swollen belly, full of life, was a constant reminder that her child's future depended on her determination. The United States was not just a destination; it was the promise of a new life, far from the shadows that had shaped her own.

Born in a humble community in Miranda state, Venezuela, Ana knew poverty from a very young age. She grew up in the slums of Caracas, where survival was the only constant. Her mother, a single woman, worked cleaning houses to feed Ana and her three younger siblings. Ana's nights were marked by uncertainty, waiting for her mother to come home to find out if there would be dinner or if they would have to go to bed hungry. Her life was a continuous struggle against hunger and need.

Ana's school uniform was a worn-out garment she wore every day, washing it when she could. Often, there was no soap at home to clean the clothes, and her mother had to wash it with just water, giving it an unmistakable smell. At school, her classmates nicknamed her "La Maloliente" ("The Smelly One") because of the rancid odor that emanated from her uniform. During recess, Ana watched with envy as other children enjoyed hot empanadas and fresh juices, while she made do with a stale piece of bread—or sometimes nothing at all. The hunger gnawed at not only her stomach but also her spirit, and Ana, without understanding economics, couldn't comprehend why others had what she did not.

The teasing wasn't limited to the cafeteria. In class, when materials were required that her mother couldn't afford, Ana arrived empty-handed, facing the laughter of her classmates and the indifference of her teachers. Low grades became a constant, not due to lack of intelligence, but because of the lack of resources. Poverty invaded her mind, trapping her in a cycle of hopelessness that seemed impossible to escape. The taunts and contempt from her classmates broke her heart daily, and tears constantly marked her face.

At twelve years old, Ana dropped out of school and began selling cookies on the street to help support her siblings. This exposed her to mistreatment from many, who looked down on her for her informal work and appearance. Some days, she encountered former classmates who either ignored her or mocked her from a distance. As a child, Ana had dreamed of becoming a teacher or a doctor, but as she grew older, she found herself trapped in a routine of work and sacrifice, where every coin she earned was managed by her mother.

At sixteen, Andrés entered her life, a bus driver who won her heart on one of the routes Ana frequently took. Andrés was cold and abusive, but Ana, despite her youthful beauty and innocent spirit, found herself stuck in a relationship where shouting and beatings were the norm. Believing this was the life she was meant to live, she clung to him for many years, having grown up with such scarcity that she didn't know what abundance looked like in any aspect of life.

Seven years later, Ana became pregnant, and her world collapsed. The news brought no joy, only more violence. Andrés accused her of infidelity and rejected the child, forbidding her from seeing a doctor. Between slaps and curses, Ana's life became an endless nightmare, where fear and despair mixed with physical and emotional pain.

Amid this hell, Ana had a conversation with Raquel, her neighbor, who spoke to her about a different world: the United States. Raquel told her how her husband had crossed the Darién Gap to reach the North American country, filling Ana's mind with stories of success. That night, as Ana lay next to Andrés, she looked around the small room they called home: a dark space with a dirt floor, dirty sheets, and walls made of scraps like wood and zinc. She realized this was not where she wanted her child to grow up. She remembered her own childhood—the mockery, the hunger—and knew she would not allow her child to live the same life.

Ana knew Andrés would never acknowledge their child and feared the baby would also suffer abuse. That night, tears streamed down her face as she imagined what life in the United States might be like, how she could work and secure a better future for her child. Though she lacked the financial means, the idea of escape clung to her mind, filling her with dreams.

Two weeks later, Ana ran into Raquel on a bus, and they began talking. Raquel, carrying a bag in hand, told her she was heading to the United States to reunite with her husband. Ana, with tears in her eyes, poured her heart out to Raquel about her situation, and on an impulse, Raquel invited her to come along. With only $250 in her pocket, Ana decided to follow Raquel on a journey that would change her life forever.

On March 20, 2023, Ana and Raquel embarked on their journey into the unknown. Two women alone, burdened with fear and hope, faced a world they knew very little about. Ana, 33 weeks pregnant, weak and malnourished, began an adventure that would test not only her body but also her spirit.

A 24-hour trip on public transportation, filled with stops and delays, was the first step of their journey. From Venezuela to Colombia, the path was relatively straightforward, though full of transfers. However, the real challenge would begin in Necoclí, the starting point for crossing the Darién Gap. There, they encountered a sea of migrants, each with their own stories of struggle and hope. Scared but determined, seeing so many others with the same goal, they joined them, sharing fears and advice, preparing for the green hell that awaited them.

Before setting out on the dangerous path, Ana and Raquel stocked up on supplies: bread, cans of tuna, tortillas, fruit, and plenty of water, following the advice of those who called themselves "experts." The fear of not being adequately prepared mixed with hope, driving their steps toward an uncertain future. They boarded a boat operated by an organization that presented itself as an expert in these transfers, although the reality was much murkier. The boatmen, their faces weathered by the sun, organized the migrants efficiently, handing out tags to claim their belongings on the other side, as if their lives had been reduced to mere luggage.

Ana, who had never been on a boat before, suffered every minute of the journey. The rocking of the waves churned her stomach and awakened her worst fears. She vomited several times, feeling as if her body, weakened by pregnancy, was betraying her. Raquel, beside her, tried to remain calm, though her eyes betrayed her anxiety. They managed to get through this stage, though neither knew for sure where they were. The only thing clear was that they were on the brink of beginning the real journey.

The Darién stretched before them like a sleeping beast, waiting to devour those desperate enough to cross it. There are several routes to navigate the jungle, but they chose the one through Capurganá, drawn by the locals' apparent familiarity with it. However, Ana would soon discover that the reality was far from that first impression.

Ana's mind was filled with uncertainty; she knew little of the world, the dangers ahead, or the complexities of the geography. She was motivated only by the stories Raquel had told her, convinced it was all part of the process. Ana listened a lot but spoke little, aware that she understood very little of what surrounded her.

Raquel, on the other hand, was a smart and resourceful woman who already knew what to expect through her husband's experience. She was fully aware of the dangers they faced but withheld this information from Ana to avoid alarming her. Raquel knew Ana had a significant limitation: her advanced pregnancy and complete ignorance of the journey ahead.

The first day of walking in the jungle was long and exhausting. They trekked for eight hours, with sections where the mud reached up to their knees. Each step was a struggle, not just against nature, but also against their own strength. The jungle revealed itself as a relentless monster, with the mud acting like claws and the humidity like its breath. Ana, with her advanced pregnancy, felt that every movement was a battle to secure a better future for her child. Yet the jungle allowed no room for heroism; everything boiled down to pure survival.

With every step, Ana felt the weight of responsibility grow more tangible. Her swollen belly was a constant reminder of what was at stake. Becoming a single mother in a world full of uncertainty was an immense burden, but Ana found strength in her fear. Raquel, more than just a neighbor, had become her friend and confidante, offering comfort when fatigue and fear overwhelmed Ana.

Exhaustion was their constant companion. Ana's feet, swollen and sore, trapped in wet, dirty shoes, became an incvitable torture. The filth of the jungle marked her body, while the towering mountains seemed to mock her fragility.

Raquel was also exhausted, but she hid her fatigue to avoid discouraging Ana. She talked to everyone along the way, while Ana, ashamed, preferred not to socialize. She feared being asked about the father of her child, and even more so, why she was making this journey alone.

At the end of the first day, they arrived at a camp where they debated whether to continue or not. The fear of the unknown competed with the dread of returning to the nightmare they had left behind. They camped in a small tent, with no comfort beyond their shared company. Surrounded by other migrants, they began to form bonds, finding in shared desperation an unexpected camaraderie.

That night, the migrants encouraged each other, devising strategies for what lay ahead. Ana realized that, despite everything, they were not as alone as they had thought. Everyone there had a story, a reason for being in that green hell. In the darkness, they shared their dreams and fears. The next morning, with their bodies still aching, they rose with renewed determination.

Ana's pregnancy did not go unnoticed. Each step was a battle against time and against her own body. Despite the pain, she pressed on, her mind filled with dreams for her child's future. During every break, she spoke to her unborn baby, narrating the journey as if it were a grand adventure—a version of *Life is Beautiful* set in the jungle.

After hours of walking, they reached the second camp by nightfall. Tents stretched across the area, and the voices of migrants filled the air. Sleeping deeply was impossible; every sound echoed through the night. Ana, curled up in her tent, stroked her belly and whispered to her baby that everything was fine, that the pain in her feet was the result of the effort to give them a better life. Meanwhile, Raquel socialized with other migrants, planning the days ahead.

Finally, past midnight, the noise died down, but the silence of the jungle was more unsettling than the bustle. The trees whispered in the darkness, and the sounds of wild animals heightened the sense of fear. Ana, exhausted, closed her eyes and tried to rest, knowing that the next day would bring more challenges.

The next leg of the journey began before dawn. By 4:30 am, still tired and drowsy, the migrants were already on the move. The smell of coffee filled the air, a luxury not everyone could afford. Some were better equipped, with flashlights cutting through the darkness, while others, like Ana and Raquel, relied on following the group to avoid getting lost. They marched on until dawn found them in the middle of the path, where they quickly ate breakfast from their provisions, aware of the need to ration.

Their goal for the day was to climb the dreaded Loma de las Banderas. The path was a test of willpower; the mud clung to their feet, and the steep climbs demanded more than many could give. At times, long lines formed on the slopes, where everyone depended on the pace of those ahead. Ropes and wooden steps, placed by other migrants, were their only allies in this challenge. The jungle became a human traffic jam, where every pause was a chance to count how many were still in the group.

The hours passed, and the goal—reaching Las Banderas—seemed like a distant dream. The exhaustion was so overwhelming that all they could do was pray to God for the strength to keep going. Ana had heard of the destination, "Las Banderas," but along the way, all she saw were increasingly difficult climbs and descents, silent witnesses to the passage of countless migrants. At that moment, skin color, economic status, and education level didn't matter; everyone was united in the same struggle. The clock kept ticking, but Ana, exhausted, knew this was only the beginning of a journey that would change her life forever.

Reaching the summit of Loma de las Banderas was an almost sacred moment, a glorious respite in the midst of the odyssey. For the walkers, arriving at that point meant more than just a geographical achievement; it was the confirmation that they had overcome a test of willpower and endurance that few could imagine. Upon reaching the top, Ana, exhausted and breathless, collapsed onto the ground, no longer caring about the mud surrounding her. The dirt, which once would have caused her shame, no longer mattered. Her only priority was to gather the strength to continue.

Around her, other migrants also took a brief pause. Many pulled out their phones to capture the moment, though their smiles couldn't hide the extreme fatigue on their faces. These photos would be more than mere memories; they would be testimonies of human resilience in the face of insurmountable adversity. Although on the verge of collapse, reaching that point was a source of pride. Some, with tears in their eyes, murmured prayers of gratitude, finding in their faith a renewed source of energy for the days still ahead.

Religion became an invisible bond that united the walkers. Amid the exhaustion, words of comfort and blessing gave them an unexpected strength. Ana, though not particularly devout, found solace in the prayers of her companions. For a brief moment, the pain and despair faded, replaced by a shared sense of hope.

However, the euphoria was dampened by the harsh reality of the place. Improvised wooden crosses marked the final resting places of those who didn't survive the journey. These crosses were a chilling reminder of the thin line between life and death in the jungle. Ana couldn't help but think that, in different circumstances, one of those crosses could have been for her or Raquel. In a silent gesture of respect, she joined the prayers for the fallen, hoping they could find the peace that had been denied to them in life.

Some migrants were injured, their feet torn apart, blisters open, and bodies utterly exhausted. Though they had passed a great trial, the next stage would be just as challenging. The descent, though less grueling than the climb, brought its own dangers: steep slopes and slippery terrain. Each step could become a deadly trap. But Ana was determined. There was no time for complaints; her sole focus was reaching the end, and Raquel, sharing her determination, kept her fears to herself.

As they pressed on, the destructive impact of humanity on the jungle became evident. Abandoned items left by other walkers—clothes, shoes, plastic bags—stained the once pristine landscape. Ana watched with sadness as the traces of human desperation manifested in the degradation of nature. What was once essential had become an unbearable burden, and the jungle now bore the scars of their passage.

Ana could see how human despair had left its mark on the destruction of the natural habitat. A heavy sorrow filled her as she observed the consequences of disrupting this route. Meanwhile, the children, unaware of the horrors of the journey, played in the rivers they crossed, their laughter echoing like a distant reminder of a lost innocence. Ana watched them with a mixture of tenderness and concern. While she was grateful that her own child was still protected within her womb, she knew that soon he would face a harsh, unforgiving world. The cries of other little ones, unable to understand why they had to walk so far, begging their parents to carry them, were a constant reminder of the immense burden of the journey.

After crossing the symbolic border of "Las Banderas," where flags from various nations waved in testament to those who had already passed through, their only guide was faith. From then on, blue ribbons tied to the trees, placed by those who had traveled the path before, marked the right way. But that route also included crossing rushing rivers that threatened to sweep them away.

The journey only paused when the body could no longer carry on, leaving the migrants exposed, alone or in small groups, far from the camps, forcing them to find inadequate spots to spend the night. Ana and Raquel spent another night in the jungle, huddled in the darkness, fully aware that the worst was still to come. At dawn, though they had conquered the densest part of the route, the victory felt bittersweet.

The next day, Ana and Raquel arrived in Bajo Chiquito, a small indigenous village in Panama. Although the place was dirty and chaotic, it offered a reprieve. Migrants could get supplies, clothing, and even a place to rest before continuing. However, the atmosphere was heavy with tension. Desperation was palpable, and fights over who would move forward were common.

Resting wasn't an option for Ana and Raquel. They wanted to finish the journey as quickly as possible, and getting out of the jungle was their most immediate goal. They spent the night there, waiting for the next leg of their trip: a four-hour ride in a dugout canoe to the UN post. The Panamanian side of the Darién Gap revealed itself as the most inhospitable part of the jungle. While Colombia had offered small oases of rest, Panama did not. The stretch was longer and crueler, and as Ana recounted her story to other migrants, she realized her memories were fragmented, difficult to piece together into a coherent narrative. The trauma had distorted her perception of time and space, and everything boiled down to one simple fact: she had survived the worst.

Finally, Ana and Raquel arrived at the UN post. The relief of reaching a safe place was overwhelming. They embraced each other in tears, feeling their bodies could take no more. They had witnessed the worst of humanity and nature: bodies along the path, eighteen people who had not survived, many left behind, unable to continue. But they had been disciplined and knew that their exhaustion couldn't defeat them.

One of the friends they had made along the way had disappeared, and the uncertainty of his fate weighed heavily on their hearts. The time it took for each migrant to reach their destination varied, but Ana and Raquel knew one thing for sure: they wanted to continue together.

Ana's emotions were a confusing blend of relief and pain. Though she was grateful to have come this far, the weight of what she had endured and lost along the way was immense. At that moment, the reality of her journey became more tangible, and the hope for a better future was the only thing keeping her determination alive. Stories from other migrants—those bitten by snakes or who had fallen and fractured bones—filled Ana with fear, but also gratitude.

She and Raquel, though exhausted, were relatively unscathed, and for now, that was enough. Ana, gently stroking her belly, thanked God for the strength He had given her to keep going. Her pregnancy, far from being a burden, had become her emotional anchor, a constant reminder of why she was doing all of this. In her mind, the idea of turning back didn't exist. Going back had never been an option, not after everything she had sacrificed.

As they continued their journey, Ana met more people, each with a story as heartbreaking as her own. She saw mothers carrying their young children, and while she felt pity for them, she also experienced a strange sense of relief knowing that her own child was still safely protected within her. She compared her situation to that of other mothers, like the woman carrying two small children and a bag. To Ana, that woman—whose name she never learned—was the true heroine, a living testament to the human spirit's ability to endure even the most brutal challenges without succumbing to exhaustion.

§

Chapter 4

Panama

The journey to Panama begins in the Darién, although for many, this point isn't clear. Since their trek starts in Colombia, within the bounds of civilization, entering the jungle causes them to lose their sense of location. Despite the fact that much of the Darién Gap is in Panamanian territory, the walkers don't feel like they're in Panama until they reencounter civilization. Passing through such dense and overwhelming nature makes them feel as though they are nowhere at all.

Tensions among the walkers increase with every step. Fatigue, hunger, and fear create an explosive mix, and differences in walking pace become reasons for conflict. However, those traveling together learn to keep quiet during moments of greatest distress, facing their inner demons with mutual solidarity. In the jungle, everyone is equal: the doctor and the street vendor walk side by side, regardless of social status or the knowledge they hold in the outside world.

In the jungle, survival depends on cooperation. The walkers exchange the little they have; paradoxically, those with the least are often the most willing to give. A can of tuna for a piece of cracker becomes a gesture of humanity amidst the hostility of nature. Many believe that once they leave the jungle, the worst is over, but they are mistaken. Outside the jungle, the world remains a hostile place, but now they face it with the certainty of having survived the hardest part.

Most of the walkers feel they've arrived in Panama once they leave the imposing jungle and board the canoes in Bajo Chiquito, the place where they begin their journey toward the UN checkpoints. The canoe ride takes about four hours. At that United Nations checkpoint, they finally feel like they've returned to civilization and, therefore, have arrived in Panama.

At this point, Panamanian authorities exercise more visible control. The border patrol is responsible, in some cases, for recovering the bodies reported by the migrants, though retrieving them all is practically impossible. Gratitude is evident among most as they realize that, against all odds, they have managed to overcome the countless obstacles of the jungle. The migrants share their experiences: swollen rivers, rainy days, and the difficult decisions made in the jungle to survive. In many cases, the choice was between their belongings or their lives.

On the other side of the Darién Gap are those who have survived. Among them are naked children in their parents' arms, and at the first aid stations, the ailments acquired in the jungle are treated. The scars on their skin, their feet completely torn apart, insect bites, and the most serious cases—fractures or strange swellings—are visible on the bodies of the migrants.

Ana:

The jungle had not only exhausted our bodies but also left an indelible mark on our souls. Every hour spent in that place was a stark reminder of the fragility of our existence, of the daily excesses we are so accustomed to because of the security we have at home: wasting water, not valuing the roof that shelters us, the blanket that protects us from the cold. Despite always having been poor, in the jungle I was able to see my own wealth.

The weight of my belly intertwined with the weight of my life, both marked by invisible but deeply painful scars. I have suffered in one way or another my entire life, and I could think that I have never truly been happy. I remembered Andrés; I had no fond memories of him, I didn't miss him, and I didn't miss my past life either. Compared to the desolation of the jungle, the abuse from a husband who never acknowledged my child seemed almost insignificant.

Each step I took, each glance lost among the towering trees, evoked a symphony of laments in my mind. Following Raquel's advice and embarking on this journey didn't seem like a good idea when my knees threatened to give way, and the soles of my feet, destroyed by con-

stant soaking in the rivers and endless walking, raised my skin in painful blisters.

The years of suffering in my childhood paled in comparison to the magnitude of the loneliness that enveloped me in the jungle. Yet, in the midst of that internal storm, I had to invent an adventure story for my child, a tale that would be his version of our journey. This would be my life from now on: a mixture of reality and fiction to shield him from the horror of what had truly happened.

My physical exhaustion intertwined with the echoes of past blows and humiliations. Every pain, every stab of fatigue, blended with the memories of those humiliations, as if the jungle and my own history had conspired to push me to the brink of my strength. When each breath felt like it would be my last and that, if I died, I would take my child with me, I clung to him as my greatest source of inspiration. I didn't know what our life in the United States would be like, but the simple fact that he would be born there seemed enough to promise him a better future.

The silence of the jungle became a labyrinth of thoughts and sorrows, a place where, little by little, I replaced the *pain with an imagination I didn't know I had. The cries of desperation were drowned out by the whisper of the wind through the trees, and the coolness on my sweaty forehead gave me the strength I needed to keep going. The vastness of nature, in its most primitive and wild form, became my only refuge.*

I couldn't understand why we had to take this path, why it seemed that being poor was synonymous with deserving the cruelty of humanity, of being invisible to all those who didn't want to see us rise in our dreams. With indifferent governments and closed borders, there are thousands of us walking hidden and in fear. I didn't know what I had done to deserve this fate, why these countries denied me legal entry, or why my life had pushed me to make a decision that led me to this point of uncertainty.

I didn't understand the reasons behind the policies that forced us to take such dangerous routes, nor did I know why life had decided I was strong enough to walk aimlessly, pregnant, toward an uncertain future. I didn't know which part of this journey would be the easiest or the hardest, nor how our life would unfold in the United States, but at this point, all I could do was keep moving forward.

After so many days since this journey began, I've lost track of how long I've been away from home. But I've also discovered something deeper: I never had a true home. Even though I lived in an urbanized area, my house was like the jungle—a place filled with sorrows and discomforts. Yet at this point, I feel stronger and wiser than the Ana who left Venezuela. The jungle changes you, pushing you to an extreme you've never experienced before, taking you to the edge where your own suffering seems insignificant compared to that of others. In the face of those who lose their loved ones on this journey, or those we leave behind, knowing they will die because no one can help them, my problems shrink.

The four hours in the dugout canoe feel easy and pass quickly for those who have already survived the Darién Gap. Complaining at this point seems illogical because you're already back in civilization—an indigenous one, but a priceless companionship in the middle of nowhere. This fragile wooden boat, with its rudimentary motor, feels like a five-star luxury simply because it saves us from more steps. This small vessel would carry us out of the heart of the jungle. Those hours, broken only by the sound of the water and the hum of insects, felt like an embrace of life. The fear was palpable, a shadow enveloping everyone. Some managed to sleep—an inconceivable feat for me, as terror and exhaustion conspired to keep me awake.

The dugout dropped us off at Puerto El Limón, a name that sounded sweet but, for us, only marked the next step in our journey. A bus waited to take us to the UN camp, for two dollars per ticket—a small sum compared to the 40 to 60 dollars it would cost for the next bus, the one that would take us to the Costa Rican border.

This trip, roughly fourteen hours long, was a physical and emotional challenge for many of us, already at the edge of our endurance. Every stage of this journey seemed designed to remind us that being a migrant was not a right, but a costly and painful privilege. We, the rejected by the world, go unnoticed by those who don't want to see us because the truth is, this path is far more crowded than the news would have you believe. But the worst part is that, along this torturous journey, we spend far more money than what it would cost for a plane ticket with the comforts of a flight.

Our poverty fuels unbalanced systems, allowing criminals and the corrupt to perpetuate this cycle. Politi-

cians talk about closing borders, but the real problem lies in their desire to silence us, in their refusal to acknowledge what is happening in the south, what drives us to look toward the north.

As I left the jungle behind, I felt a mix of relief and triumph. It was as if I had won a prize for enduring. That prize was mine, and only mine. I had discovered so many hidden abilities in the midst of this hardship, and it was my inner strength that allowed me to keep going and not give up, even though my inner thighs were completely raw from the constant chafing of my legs. Despite the doubts others had about me, despite my body seeming ready to give up more than once due to my advanced pregnancy and the extra weight, I had made it to the other side.

The weight of the belongings I had carried for days became insignificant in the face of the desire to keep moving forward. I remembered my mother's words, urging me to eat when I was a child, telling me that many people in the world were starving. At that moment, those words took on a terrifyingly real meaning. It was said that many of the deceased we encountered had died from lack of food.

I firmly believe that for us, leaving Panama is an act of desperation, as the Panamanian jungle leaves deep scars. That's why our time in Panama City was brief.

Upon arriving in Ciudad de David, I felt something inside me break, as though the last strands of strength keeping me upright unraveled. The physical exhaustion was overwhelming, but what weighed on me most was the emotional burden I had carried since setting foot in the Darién. As soon as I stepped off the bus, a stranger with a kind yet penetrating gaze approached me and called out. His voice, though warm, filled me with fear—perhaps due to the heightened survival instincts honed in the jungle or the distrust I had developed during the journey.

My appearance spoke for itself; I didn't need to tell my story because my face and movements already told it all. When I saw the bag of bread and soft drinks he offered, all the pain, anguish, and despair I had held back for days spilled out in the form of tears. I had thought humanity had faded in the jungle, but this gesture reminded me that there are still good people in the world.

The taste of a simple ham sandwich, something so basic yet so meaningful, brought me back to life. I felt my baby move inside me, as if sharing my relief, as if that small act of generosity had given him the strength I had lost. We spent the night in Ciudad de David, a refuge amidst the storm. But the next day, reality hit us again: we had to continue toward the border with nowhere to stay.

Worry crept back in when an older woman approached, sensing our state of mind. She invited us to spend the night at her house, something I couldn't believe after everything we had been through. This woman, a former Red Cross worker, offered her home without hesitation. She allowed us to bathe, a luxury we hadn't had in days, and prepared a hot dinner. As we ate, she shared stories of the migrants she had helped and how she had seen the hell of the Darién reflected in their eyes. To her, those who managed to cross the jungle were given a divine blessing, a promise of a better future. I don't know if that's true, but the fact that she took us in already felt like a miracle.

There are many groups that help migrants along their journey, and we owe these kind-hearted people our gratitude. They perform a noble service, but often, they cannot fully understand what it means to us, those who have endured the great passage of the Darién.

Each survival story from the jungle is unique, and every person carries a burden of indescribable experiences. For some, the deepest pain came from seeing the lifeless bodies of those who didn't survive; for others, it was the exhaustion lodged in every muscle, a fatigue so intense it seemed to drain the soul.

In the Darién, the sense of loneliness is overwhelming, an unsettling paradox when you find yourself surrounded by other walkers. We traveled through that jungle because it was the only path left to us; governments had denied us the right to cross their lands through regular means, imposing invisible barriers that failed to understand the pain and desperation of those seeking a better life.

But amidst that desolate emptiness, sometimes humanity reveals itself in unexpected ways. It's like a warm embrace for the soul when you encounter generous hearts who, without knowing the harshness of the Darién, extend their hands with food and water, illuminating our path with a flicker of humanity. Every act of solidarity, despite borders and differences, reminds us that, after all, we share the same space in this world.

The people who help us do so without seeking recognition or reward. We, who have experienced their kindness, are grateful for their existence with every fiber of our being. Amid the confusion and uncertainty, those hands offering us food and water become tangible displays of solidarity that transcend languages and cultures. Every shared meal is a message of support, a sign that we are not alone in our journey, and that, despite the adversity, there is still light on the path and human beings willing to ease the weight of our burden.

These acts of generosity, though anonymous, leave an indelible mark on our lives. The people who share what little they have with us, weaving a network of compassion, embrace us in the moments we need it most. They remind us that even in the vastness of the jungle, we are not completely alone, and that after every storm, no matter how fierce, calm always follows.

As I lay in the comfort of a bed, my mind couldn't stop traveling back to those days in the jungle. Over and over again, like a persistent echo, the memories assaulted me, filling me with a sadness I couldn't shake. I thought of the endless hours when I dragged my feet along paths that challenged my knees, enduring five days of hardship in the midst of a hostile and unfor-

giving nature. That place, forgotten by man, seemed determined to remain untouched, like a natural barrier dividing the north from the south.

§

Chapter 5
Costa Rica

Each country along this journey is much more than just a name on a map; it is a challenge and a goal that every migrant must overcome, and success can only be achieved through organization, determination, and a well-planned strategy. At this stage, migrants have an even clearer objective: to reach the United States as quickly as possible.

Borders, far from being mere dividing lines, represent both promises and threats. Without knowledge of the laws or concern for time, the routes remain a mystery, and each step is taken without any certainty. At this point, migrants begin to face dangers of human origin, far greater than those they had previously encountered. Now they are illegal immigrants, not always welcomed as they move forward.

Costa Rica, known as "the happiest country in the world," seems to live up to that reputation in the reality experienced by migrants. The crossing from Panama was surprisingly easy, almost as if they were being invited in without much questioning. A shared taxi took the group for two long hours to a bus terminal. In this country, migrants find public restrooms where they can freshen up without needing to pay for a hotel, allowing them to regain some dignity. Many also spend the night in bus terminals, as Costa Rica proves to be an expensive country, imposing a brief stay for most.

Spending a night in the capital at a cost of ten dollars per person is an unnecessary expense for the majority, so many choose to continue their journey without stopping. Most of these migrants have limited resources to reach their final destination, which drives them to push forward, even when the exhaustion weighs heavily on them.

Raquel:

In Costa Rica, it became necessary to pause and sleep in a hotel, especially due to Ana's exhaustion. Despite her strength, the weight of her silence was becoming suffocating. I often wondered why she didn't speak, why she had remained quiet for most of the journey, reflecting a deep pain she didn't dare share. Ana's resilience suggested that her previous life must have been a living hell, but the questions about her motivations stayed trapped in my mind, fearing they might reopen wounds too deep to heal.

My husband had suggested we spend a night in Costa Rica, and I also needed to find money, as I had almost run out. I felt responsible for Ana; after all, I was the one who invited her on this journey, knowing she didn't have the necessary resources.

He had already warned me about crossing into Nicaragua—a new challenge filled with anxiety and fear. This border had been dangerous for him in the past, but I didn't want to share anything tragic with Ana to avoid worrying or stressing her further. I felt the need to protect her, especially because there was a connection between us, though not one built on deep trust. It was more of an instinctive need to shield her and her pregnancy.

Before we left, my husband gave me the contact of a man who owned a hotel where we could spend the night, rest, eat, and prepare for the next leg of our journey.

In the hotel's kitchen, I met Manuel, who also planned to cross into Nicaragua the next day. We connected immediately. We started talking about the remaining part of the journey, the routes ahead, the budget, and logistical details. Our conversation lasted several hours, and I liked him from the start.

I had left Venezuela with Ana, and neither of us had ever emigrated before. Hearing the story of someone in a similar situation, but who had already lived in another country, was something new to me. I asked Manuel where he came from, and he replied:

—I started my journey in Ecuador, where I lived for the last four years. I didn't begin this trip alone; at first, there were four of us: two Venezuelans and two Ecuadorians, young and full of the arrogance that only youth can offer. We thought the Darién would be an easy test, just another obstacle we would overcome without much trouble. However, we quickly

realized that the Darién wasn't just a physical trial; it was a mental challenge, a confrontation with our deepest fears."

Manuel continued:

—In Ecuador, I worked in a bar, earning just enough to live in a small room. However, my boss, a bitter and cruel man, treated me with disdain for being Venezuelan, constantly reminding me that I was nothing more than a floor cleaner, a foreigner in his country. Over time, I came to understand that being a foreigner meant learning to endure, to work harder, because there was no other choice. Those experiences, though tough, prepared me for the future, teaching me how to survive with little and to keep moving forward with whatever I had.

He paused, then added:

—I managed to save six thousand dollars while living in Ecuador, but the death of my mother changed everything. I received the news like a devastating blow. I couldn't return to Venezuela to say goodbye to her. My sister suggested that it was better to remember her as she was in life, rather than face the emptiness

of her absence. Although those words hurt me deeply, I understood she was right: my mother was no longer there, and going back wouldn't change that reality.

Manuel spoke with a restrained sadness, as if retelling the story over and over had worn down the emotions, but his words touched us deeply. I could imagine what it would be like to lose my own parents from afar, without the chance to say goodbye. Manuel continued his story:

—There wasn't a single day that my mother didn't send me a message wishing me the best. Many times, I would get irritated and not respond, never realizing how short our time together would be. The day she passed, she sent me a message saying she wasn't feeling well, but hoped we would see each other soon. I replied with a promise I couldn't keep, not knowing it would be our last conversation. Even though she was only sixty-one, she passed away suddenly from a heart attack. From that moment, I realized that sometimes, the good ones are called away too soon.

With a trembling voice, Manuel confessed:

—I feel an immense guilt for not being with her in her final years. It hurts that I couldn't give her the farewell she deserved. I emigrated in search of a better future, but in the process, I lost the most valuable things: her sincere embrace, those loving good mornings, the warm arepa and coffee with milk in the mornings. My heart broke the day I realized I would never receive anything from my mother again. I'm ashamed that I didn't help her more, and that I lied to her so many times. She always dreamed of seeing me return, and I feel like I failed her. But I also know I have nothing left to return to in Venezuela. My mother walks with me in every step; she's my angel and my blessing.

Despite his story, Manuel kept a smile on his face. His positive energy radiated around him, which was surprising, considering all that he had been through. Perhaps, as he had suggested, it is in adversity that one truly finds their inner strength.

So, the next morning, we agreed to leave the hotel with Manuel at 4:30 a.m., heading toward Nicaragua.

§

Charter 6
Nicaragua

To reach Nicaragua from Costa Rica, they had to cross a small river by boat, and on the other side, they were met with a walk along a dirt road that, due to the rain, was flooded and covered in mud. Seeing the mud, Raquel felt memories from the past overwhelm her mind. The nightmare of the Darién, which she thought she had left behind, resurfaced with force. The episodes she had lived through in the jungle had turned into traumas that were now manifesting as anxiety attacks.

Until that moment, the presence of Ana and Manuel had brought her comfort, but as she stepped into the thick mud, the demons she believed she had conquered came back to haunt her. She remembered how the rain had turned the Darién path into a treacherous quagmire, and the memories emerged with painful clarity. The Darién was no longer a simple memory, but a living, oppressive reality in her mind. What was most strange to Raquel was the terror she felt now, a fear she had never experienced before.

In her mind, the cries of children desperate from hunger and exhaustion echoed, along with the abandoned bodies they had encountered. Everything swirled together in a whirlwind that threatened to consume her sanity. She walked, crying, feeling how each step sank her deeper into the mud, both physically and emotionally, into her own fears.

She turned to look at Ana, who, as always, seemed calm. Ana maintained a tranquility that unsettled Raquel. At first glance, Ana's apparent indifference contrasted with Raquel's own desperation. The mud clinging to Raquel's skin was a reminder of all they had lost and what they could still lose. They were not safe, nor anywhere near their destination. The trails and hidden paths they had to traverse were far from over.

As Raquel walked, her mind drifted back to Venezuela, to those days when she had fought for change. The hope she once had had faded, forcing her husband to leave the country, leaving her alone and unprotected. What remained in her heart was a deep hatred for the government that had forced them to flee. She had left behind the house she had built with so much effort, block by block, chasing an American dream she wasn't sure even existed.

Her husband spoke to her about opportunities in the United States, though he made it clear that nothing would be easy. They didn't speak English, and they knew even less about the system. However, that promise of a better life, of working and living with dignity, was the only thing keeping Raquel going. But the harsh reality of the journey was hitting her hard.

Poverty surrounded her. Everyone traveling with them was of low means from Venezuela. In her country, politicians talked about helping the poor, but it was all lies. They lived in luxury while the rest fought to survive. It was common to see politicians and their children driving the most expensive SUVs, shamelessly flaunting their wealth on social media.

The journey to Nicaragua took them through an orange grove. In the distance, a checkpoint could be seen, and they had already been warned not to cross there. The "welcome" to Nicaragua included a migration control that would charge them $150 for a travel permit, an amount they couldn't afford. To avoid it, they had to skirt around the area. After trudging through the mud, they reached a road where some houses offered bathing facilities, charging for the service.

They took a bus that drove them for hours to another location, where a different bus awaited them. At that point, confusion set in—they didn't know exactly where they were. This forced them to pay a small guide to continue. It was incredible how, even in the middle of civilization, they felt more lost than they had in the jungle. Passing through immigration was a constant nightmare, with the fear of being detained and sent back haunting them.

Finally, they managed to reach Managua without being stopped, giving them a sigh of relief. They stayed in a hotel that night, exhausted but thankful. For the first time, Raquel saw Ana break down. She had always been the strong one, but now she was exhausted, and her pregnancy was taking its toll. Ana felt pain in her belly and a deep physical discomfort.

Raquel, worried, sought help and discovered that the hotel owner was a nurse. She voluntarily examined Ana and, after a brief conversation, noticed that Ana had gone through her pregnancy without any medical care. She hadn't taken any medicines or vitamins, and in recent weeks, she had been poorly nourished. The extreme exertion of walking through the Darién had completely drained her body.

They had to spend three days resting at that place. During those days, they saw other migrants arrive, each with their own story of struggle and faith. Manuel didn't leave them; he stayed with them, as they had formed an incredible bond.

One of those nights, while they were talking, Manuel decided to share his story, a tale filled with sadness that revealed why he was alone when they first met him

Manuel:

From the beginning, we knew the journey would be hard, but no one was truly prepared for what we would face in the Darién. We embarked on the journey united by a common goal: to reach the United States. However, the Darién is a place that separates the strong from the weak, the brave from the desperate. Every step was a reminder of human fragility and the inner strength needed to keep going.

The first two days, we walked together, the four of us, but soon we realized that each person had their own pace and way of dealing with adversity. We tried to stay united, but the harshness of the environment eroded even the best intentions. Along the path, we saw many people struggling, especially mothers with children and those who had never faced such a physically demanding challenge. We helped many along the way, especially the children, whose faces reflected a fear and exhaustion that were difficult to bear.

Among us was Martín, a long-time friend, but also the weakest in the group. From the beginning, he lagged behind more than the rest, always complaining and doubting. Though we all faced our fears, Martín seemed to be constantly on the verge of giving up. We made the most of every hour of daylight, fearing the night, when the jungle became even more terrifying.

On the third day, Martín woke up with his foot swollen, painful, and misshapen, with no apparent explanation. From that moment on, he became a burden. In addition to the pain in his foot, he began to develop a fever, and every step became torture for both him and us. The torrential rain and treacherous terrain only worsened the situation.

We decided to carry him, improvising a stretcher with sticks and a sheet. We took turns carrying him, though in that green hell, there was no real rest. The rain beat down on us mercilessly, and the mud made us slip with every step. The mountains were steep and dangerous, and each descent was a struggle to maintain our balance.

During one of my rest shifts, I watched my friends as they tried to carry Martín up a particularly steep part of the trail. The slippery ground and the sheer force of nature overwhelmed them, and in an instant, they disappeared over the edge of the cliff. I screamed, but my voice was drowned out by the roar of the rain and the wind. There was no response, only the relentless sound of nature.

I lost my friends that day, and with them, a part of myself. The moment I saw them fall, I knew there was no turning back. I stood there, frozen in horror, as the world crumbled around me. Yet, amid the tragedy, I felt a strange calm, a certainty that could only come from my mother, who had always protected me, even from beyond the grave. Somehow, I knew she had kept me from being the one who fell. But now I was alone.

Manuel's words left Raquel stunned. She had never imagined the depth of the suffering he had endured on this journey. His story was filled with a pain so profound that she could barely process it. Every word etched itself into her mind, resonating with the harshness of a reality they had tried to avoid but that had always lingered nearby. She didn't know what to say. What could she possibly express in the face of such a confession of loss and guilt? Words escaped her, as if the wind carried them away before they could form on her lips. She looked at him, trying to convey through her eyes the empathy she felt, the understanding she couldn't put into words.

The silence between them at that moment was heavy, but necessary. No more words were needed; his pain had said it all.

Finally, Raquel broke the silence and told Manuel that she would find something to prepare soup for Ana. She knew they needed to busy their hands and minds with something practical, something to pull them back to the immediate reality and away, if only for a moment, from the ghosts Manuel had just summoned. Raquel didn't want to imagine what he had seen or experienced in the Darién, nor did she want to revisit the desperation of her own panic attacks.

They headed to the small kitchen the hotel provided for its guests, where other migrants were cooking with the little they had. The air was filled with familiar smells, though strange in a place so far from home. While their stories were different, they all shared the same struggle. It was a fragile comfort, but in that moment, any comfort was welcome.

They prepared the soup in silence, working together in a wordless choreography that required no conversation. As Raquel stirred the broth, her thoughts drifted to Ana, to her quiet strength, and how they were all carrying more weight than they should, both physically and emotionally. The soup was a small gesture, but in this context, it meant so much. It was their way of caring for one another, offering a bit of comfort despite everything they had lost.

When the soup was ready, they returned to the room. Ana was lying down, one hand resting on her belly, her eyes closed as she tried to block out the pain. The worry on her face was clear, but when she saw them enter with the soup, she managed a small smile, grateful for their effort.

Manuel, who had been silent throughout the preparation, approached her and, with a gentleness that surprised Raquel, asked,

—Ana, where is the baby's father?

The question hung in the air for a moment, and Ana's expression shifted, as if the question had touched a sensitive nerve. Slowly, she began to speak, her voice low and laden with memories. And so, another story began to unfold, full of pain, difficult decisions, and a love that had not been enough to protect her from all that the world had thrown at her. Raquel had never dared to ask much about Ana's past, but Manuel, new to their lives, was curious.

Ana:

I left Venezuela carrying the weight of a life that had always crushed me. It wasn't a choice, but a desperate need to escape a reality that was suffocating me. Now, as I speak to you, the pain sharpens with every word. If I were to tell you everything that brought me here, you'd probably prefer not to know any of it, nor about Andrés, the man who claimed to love me.

Andrés always found ways to make me feel small and insignificant. He said this baby wasn't his, as if that justified the horror with which he treated me. Every day brought a new form of control, a new humiliation. He degraded me, and at night, he forced me to satisfy his desires as if my body belonged to him. His love was a prison I couldn't escape, and his sickening jealousy was the chain that kept me trapped in that dark reality.

Raquel, my neighbor, spoke to me about a new life in the United States. I ran into her by chance, just when she was about to start her own journey. I don't know if it was fate or a cruel joke of life, but there she was, offering me a chance to escape. But as I crossed the green hell of the Darién, I wondered if I had made the right choice. Was the terror of living with Andrés worse, or was it the abyss of the unknown? Sometimes, I still don't know.

My life has always been marked by misery. Since I was a child, poverty was my only companion. I never knew what it was like to have more, to dream of a different future. Ignorance enveloped me, and I wasn't aware of the world beyond my borders. Everything changed when I found out I was pregnant. Inside me grew a reason, a purpose I had never known before: to protect my baby and take it far away from the shadow of my fate.

This child won't be like me. They won't be someone life tramples over, the way it has with me. It doesn't matter if it's a boy or a girl; their future will be bright. If it's a boy, I imagine him as an engineer, building a world I could never have imagined. If it's a girl, perhaps she'll be a doctor, saving lives instead of just surviving, as I've done.

Each step I took in the Darién brought me closer to that goal, but also confronted me with new suffering, a pain that revealed just how cruel life can be. I heard stories that made mine seem insignificant, tales of despair and loss that made me realize that perhaps life doesn't hate me; it's simply relentless. And yet, I keep moving forward, because this baby I carry inside is my hope, my promise that pain is not the only thing that exists in the world.

I don't know if you ever met Silvia. Three guerrillas raped her in front of her twelve-year-old daughter. When Silvia told me her story, she did so with a strange mix of pride and resignation, as if being raped instead of her daughter was a triumph. For her, the sacrifice of her body was a price she was willing to pay to protect what she loved most. I understood then that the hell I lived through with Andrés, although brutal, was insignificant compared to what Silvia had endured.

Andrés treated me as if I were nothing more than an extension of his will. He said it was his duty as a man, and my obligation as his wife, to satisfy him regardless of my desires. He practically raped me, because when you don't want it and don't enjoy it, that's what it is—rape. I clung to the idea that I loved him, because he was my husband, because he had convinced me that this was love. Today, I know it wasn't.

I don't want to, nor can I, imagine what is now hidden in Silvia's daughter's mind after witnessing the brutality against her mother. That kind of pain leaves scars that never heal. It terrifies me to think that if Andrés ever discovers where I went, he might try to drag me back to his side. But I am determined: he will never know. And if he ever finds out, I'll be so far away that his shadow won't be able to reach me.

Escaping the prison that was my life with Andrés was the first step. Now I want more. I want to study, to learn, to be something more than a victim. I've left behind the woman who was content with just surviving, and I'm determined never to return to that prison. Moving forward, even though it's painful, is the only option I have left.

During this journey, we met people who, like us, carried their own stories of pain and resilience. I want this to one day be just a memory, an anecdote in my life and in my baby's life. I want to be able to tell my child that we overcame this together, that all the suffering was worth it because it led us to a better place.

Today, the exhaustion and pain weigh on me, but tomorrow will be a new day. The Darién taught me more about myself than I ever imagined. I discovered that I'm much stronger than I thought, that I don't need anyone to define me, and that, even though the road is hard, I have the strength to walk it. What awaits me at the end of this journey is freedom, and that's something worth fighting for.

I let Andrés hit me because, for so long, I thought he was stronger than me. His violence and aggression seemed like proof of a power I believed I didn't have.

But now, after everything I've been through, I can see how wrong that thinking was. Andrés, with all his machismo and cruelty, wouldn't last a day on the journey I've made. Maybe that's what gave me the strength to keep going: the thought that I would never have to see him again, that I could finally leave him behind.

Life is just one, and every story I've heard in that jungle has shown me that when you have a dream, you must chase it, no matter the obstacles. That's how I listened to your story, Manuel, when you told Raquel about your mother. At some point, your story made me feel like I had made the right decision to come here with my baby. I don't want, one day, to be in your mother's place, longing to see her son who left in search of an opportunity in another country.

I know that right now, my own mother must be suffering in the same way yours did. But my priority is my child, my only companion in this life. I'm with Raquel, it's true, but she has her husband and her family. When I get there, I need to find a way to build a life for myself and for my baby. I need to do what I've never done: live for myself, for us, and not for anyone else.

When my son grows up, if he's a boy, I want him to be like you, Manuel. I want him to take care of every woman he meets along his path, to not be a brute like his father. Life has values that must be taught, and I'm sure your mother taught you to be a gentleman, to respect and protect others. Andrés, on the other hand, never had that chance. His mother abandoned him, and it left a wound in him that never healed. That abandonment turned him into someone full of hatred toward women, unable to see them as anything more than objects to use and discard.

To Andrés, there is no good woman; we are all garbage, something to be stomped on without remorse. But deep down, I understood something about him: all that hatred, all that cruelty, are reflections of the pain he carries inside. It's his way of dealing with an internal demon he could never defeat. I've also had to face my own demons, but now, with my son as my reason, I know I can be stronger than they are. Andrés never understood that, and that's why his life is destined to be a chain of destruction. I, on the other hand, am determined to break that cycle, to be different, to build a future where love and respect prevail, for me and for my child.

In Nicaragua, immigrants discover that kindness can bloom in the most unexpected places. The people there are humble, but what little they have, they share with a generosity that isn't found everywhere. While immigrants wait on the streets, it's common for someone to approach with a bottle of water or a bit of food, as if they understand the enormity of the journey they are undertaking. It's as if they know, deep down, that this journey is not just a physical passage, but a fight for hope and survival.

Leaving Nicaragua isn't easy. To get to Jalapa, the trip takes more than six hours, and on every bus we took, we found other migrants who, like us, had crossed the Darién jungle. We saw mothers holding their children in their arms, entire families who had left everything behind, and many people traveling alone. Raquel often thought that she couldn't imagine what it would be like to take this journey alone, without anyone to share the fear and hope.

On one of the buses we took, we met Sofía, who had started her journey in Valencia, Venezuela, with her two young children, one three years old and the other five. Sofía told us that, in the darkness of the jungle, an animal bit her eldest son. She thinks it was a snake or a spider. Without access to medical care, the boy quickly deteriorated. For two days, she carried him in her arms, battling his fever and convulsions. When they finally reached a Red Cross camp, it was already too late. The venom had done its work, and the boy didn't survive.

Despite this immeasurable pain, Sofía didn't stop. With tears in her eyes, but with incredible strength, she decided to continue the journey with her youngest son. Her pain was evident, her swollen eyes showed she cried often, living with an indescribable sorrow. Yet, with her child in her arms, Sofía was the embodiment of strength, a mother who, despite having lost so much, continued fighting for the child she still had.

When we arrived in Jalapa, we found ourselves in a humble, simple village. We were exhausted and hungry, but there was no time to stop and look for food. The border was almost two hours away, and every hour mattered.

On this journey, time is a luxury we can't afford in some stretches. There are steps that must be taken by day and others by night, and any delay could mean missing an opportunity or facing a greater danger. We couldn't spend money on hotels, so most migrants sleep in bus terminals, where danger lurks at every corner, but the fact that it's free is enough to motivate them to take the risk. Without any comforts, few people truly rest, and they take turns watching over each other.

When we reached the border at 'Las Manos,' we were met with a crowd of people who, like us, were trying to leave Nicaragua and enter Honduras. For those who are undocumented, each border crossing is a battle.

However, on this occasion, luck was on our side, and we didn't run into any problems. They let us pass, and in that moment, we felt like we had overcome another obstacle on our way toward an uncertain future.

Ana, with her advanced pregnancy, became a symbol of hope for everyone. At times, it seemed her condition acted like a charm, helping us navigate the challenges of the journey. People offered her water, gave her help, and in those small gestures, others saw that even in the darkest moments, humanity can shine brightly. This journey is a test of endurance, but it's also a lesson in the human capacity for kindness and solidarity, even in the midst of adversity.

§

Charter 7
Honduras

For migrants, crossing the border into Honduras offers a brief moment of relief, which quickly turns into a tense situation. There's a heavy air, and the stories about the country are far from encouraging. The suffocating heat mixes with the desperation to leave those lands as quickly as possible.

To cross Honduras, migrants need a "Salvoconducto," a document granting them legal passage for a specified amount of time. They have five days to cross the country and avoid deportation. Time becomes the enemy of bad decisions.

The process of obtaining the Salvoconducto translates into a long line, several hours of waiting, where all those trying to comply with the law gather to avoid trouble. Their exhausted faces reflect their fears and anxieties. By then, many have been away from home for over fifteen days, far from any comforts or long rest, and some have barely eaten properly. Yet, in the midst of that wait, the barriers of silence break down, and stories begin to be shared.

It's in those conversations that the diversity of accents becomes clear. It's not just Venezuelans on the road to the American dream; there are also people from Ecuador, Peru, and Colombia, all driven by the same desperation and the hope for a better life. It's striking to see how many Venezuelans are in the same situation. They weren't the only ones, but the majority of those present were from Venezuela. In those talks, migrants shared their hardships and the reasons pushing them north: the lack of security, limited opportunities, and the blatant corruption in their home countries.

A common factor among them is that they are people of low means. There are no traces of luxury in their clothes or shoes, which are completely worn out, not just from crossing the Darién, but from the hardships of a difficult life. They all gamble on finding something better in the unknown.

The similarity in their stories is remarkable: people who sold everything they had to embark on the journey, with a small bag as their only luggage. They know they still have a long way to go, and with the hope of staying connected, they exchange phone numbers. Among them, there are no professionals or wealthy individuals; they are not common on this path.

Many share the feeling of being treated like criminals throughout the journey. All they want is to reach the United States.

Receiving the Salvoconducto is a relief, but also a reminder that they are unwanted in these territories. The limited time on the document is merely a temporary green light to continue on their way.

However, amid that institutional coldness, there are flashes of humanity. In Honduras, there are shelters for migrants passing through, where they are offered a bed to rest and food to eat. Those who lack sufficient resources deeply appreciate these gestures. After so many hardships, any act of kindness is cherished, but it also serves as a reminder of the harsh reality they are living.

The Hondurans are remembered as kind people who understand the pain of migrants. Many have relatives in the United States and share similar stories of migration and dreams. The Honduran people have endured political and economic crises, and while they don't face the challenge of crossing the Darién, they understand that the journey ahead for the migrants is even tougher.

In these shelters, migrants are given what they might need to continue their journey. Ana was given medicine, folic acid, and special food for pregnant women. The next day, they had to continue, taking a bus to Tegucigalpa that would leave early in the morning to make the most of daylight. The journey took three hours, but at least they could be at ease, knowing they had legal permission to travel through the country.

Along the way, it's common to encounter police checkpoints, where officers check the migrants to ensure they have the Salvoconducto. Those without the document are taken off the bus and sent back. However, even those with proper permits are not always safe from extortion by the police, who often ask for small "contributions" to let them continue. Out of fear, migrants often comply.

During these long journeys, it's common for migrants to share conversations and get to know one another. The routes are well-traveled by those seeking to cross the country, and they often encounter others who are also searching for a future in the north.

Ana:

This time, I sat next to a fourteen-year-old boy named Rubén, who was traveling with his father. Despite his young age, Rubén carried the weight of an adult. His demeanor could easily deceive anyone, making him appear older, but in his voice and words, the innocence of a child still shone through.

Rubén began telling me about his life in Caracas, in a humble home in Petare, where he lived with his grandmother. From a young age, he had worked alongside his father, selling snacks on the streets and buses. He had also worked in markets, packing groceries, cleaning windows, and even performing juggling tricks at traffic lights. Despite the hard lessons life had imposed on him, Rubén still had a spark of dreams in his eyes. With a touching simplicity, he shared with me his longing for a dignified Christmas. For him, Christmas represented more than just a holiday; it was the hope of receiving something more than disappointments. He wanted children, like himself, to have the chance to experience a Christmas without broken toys or unfulfilled promises.

His vision of the United States was almost utopian: a place where meals would never be scarce, where hous-

es and cars would be within anyone's reach. He spoke as if his future was already written in prosperity. The clarity with which he described his goals, despite his youth, showed a maturity shaped by necessity. He was such a dreamer that his innocence enveloped him, as if the stories he had heard from others were fueling that hope.

His life in Venezuela was marked by poverty. He hadn't attended school, but he knew enough to make a living. His practical intelligence, born out of experience, was his greatest asset. When he mentioned his mother, his tone changed, filled with deep affection. Together with his father, they had decided she couldn't make the journey due to her fragile health, but they promised her they would bring her by plane once they had saved enough money.

Rubén saw his mother as a queen, a woman who, despite adversity, had been the pillar of his life. His greatest desire was to work and send her money, to help her fix the teeth she had lost during her pregnancy. His affection for his mother and grandmother was constant, even during the hardest times.

He wanted to send them money for medicine and to repair the dilapidated shack they lived in. The reality *of his life in Venezuela, with a house that flooded when it rained and food always scarce, contrasted with his dream of a better future in the United States. His resourcefulness in finding food on the streets, whether by asking for it or scavenging through trash, reminded me of my own childhood.*

Rubén had learned to accept death with a frankness that sent chills down my spine. He recounted his passage through the Darién with an incredible laugh, but that laugh was a shield against the horrors he had experienced. The jungle hadn't broken his spirit. He had learned to move forward, to seize every opportunity, like finding an abandoned tent rather than spending money on his own.

Rubén smiled with the satisfaction of someone who had learned to live with little and appreciate the essentials. For him, finding an abandoned tent wasn't just luck— it was a lifeline in the middle of nowhere. Every time he spoke, I could feel his father's words resonate within him. The admiration he had for his father was palpable: a mix of respect and love forged in the tough streets of Caracas.

They had worked in Costa Rica, selling sweets to save money to continue their journey. The idea of selling sweets in the United States filled him with hope. He saw himself as a "graduate" of the street vendor life, but his aspirations didn't stop there: he wanted to be a millionaire. His father was his role model, a man capable of doing anything to survive, but Rubén aspired to more. He didn't just want to survive; he wanted to thrive.

That night, we stayed in a modest hotel in Tegucigalpa. Although simple and worn down, it was a refuge for us, a place to rest for a few hours. The next day, we set off for the border at El Florido. The nearly eight-hour journey heightened our anxiety, knowing we faced a trek through difficult terrain. After crossing the Darién, any other path seemed easier, though no less daunting.

The border at El Florido was a swarm of weary people and exhausted bodies. Crossing wasn't easy, and every step seemed to take us further from the rest we so desperately longed for. The trochas, clandestine paths used by migrants to evade controls, were our only option. But these paths, guided by "trocheros" who preyed on our desperation, were expensive.

For those of us who had walked for days through the Darién, any trocha seemed easy, but each stretch was a new test, a reminder that the journey was far from over. As we pressed on, hiding along the way, I couldn't help but think about Rubén, his father, and all those like us who had left everything behind in search of a better future.

§

Charter 8
Guatemala

Ana:

Arriving in Guatemala feels like an abrupt awakening in the midst of endless green landscapes. Nature seems to welcome us with open arms, but reality hits hard. We walk along the road, each step weighing down our exhausted bodies, until we reach a migrant assistance center. Fear, our eternal companion, walks with us under the scorching sun, ever-present as we fear being discovered and sent back to the place we fought so hard to escape.

Guatemala, though seemingly welcoming, greets us with shadows. The police, vigilant in their patrols, chase us as if we were criminals, mercilessly deporting those they catch. Raquel's husband had warned us about the dangers posed by the cartels in this territory: "Trust no one; in Guatemala, the risk of being kid-

napped is real." His words echo in my mind, urging us to stay on the margins, to avoid any contact that might betray us. The police, far from being our protection, are a threat. Every step we take in this land makes us feel like fugitives, even though we haven't committed any crime. In this cruel world, being an illegal immigrant means becoming a ghost, an invisible being wandering foreign lands, trying not to leave a trace, trying not to exist.

Fear is a constant companion, one that doesn't leave with time or distance. Some countries, like Costa Rica, welcomed us with relative ease, but in others, fear becomes an unbearable burden, a shadow looming over us at every turn. We walk knowing that our very presence is a transgression in the eyes of those who claim these lands as their own. We live in a constant dance with fear, calculating every move to avoid capture, to avoid deportation.

The journey to Esquipulas, which should take an hour and a half by car, turns into a six-hour ordeal of anxiety. In the jungle, our fears were dictated by untamed nature; here, the danger is man-made. Each step brings us closer to the Casa del Migrante San José, where hope seems to fade with every passing minute, until we finally arrive, exhausted, seeking a place to rest and regain our strength. There, Mrs. Nancy greets us with a warmth that defies our expectations. Her smile and kindness become a beacon of hope amidst the darkness.

Nancy, with her tireless dedication, makes us feel welcome from the very first moment. Her shelter becomes a sanctuary, a place where hopelessness temporarily dissipates. In her presence, the hatred and distrust fade, and we can breathe, even if just for a brief moment, without the weight of paranoia on our shoulders. Nancy shows us that kindness knows no borders and that, in every corner of the world, no matter how inhospitable it may seem, there are people willing to extend a helping hand.

But Guatemala remains a land of contrasts. In our minds, two images emerge: the dangerous Guatemala, dominated by cartels and corruption, and the humane Guatemala, represented by people like Nancy. It's a duality reflected in every step we take, in every glance we exchange. We cannot ignore the dangers surrounding us, but neither can we forget the kindness we've encountered along the way.

The next day, we took a bus to Guatemala City, a journey that should have been straightforward, but soon turned into another ordeal. From the window, we watched the changing landscapes, but the trip, which was supposed to last five hours, was abruptly interrupted when the driver, after charging us $25, abandoned us almost two hours away from our destination, leaving us stranded. We were easy prey for those looking to take advantage of our vulnerability. As illegal migrants, our voices are silenced by fear, unable to report the abuses we suffer.

From Guatemala City, we took another bus toward the Hidalgo border, the entry point to Mexico. The nearly seven-hour journey was marked by several police stops, where we were repeatedly forced to pay bribes. During those endless hours, we made two bathroom stops, and at each, we encountered more migrants. One question kept circling in my mind: Why are there so many of us? What drives us to leave everything behind and face such an uncertain, dangerous path?

At the terminal, before boarding the bus to Guatemala City, we met Claudia and Ernesto, a couple whose youth radiated a mix of hope and melancholy. They were from San Cristóbal, a place that seemed so distant amid our pilgrimage. They were young, likely in their twenties, and while their faces reflected the innocence typical of their age, their eyes carried the shadow of those who had lived too much in too little time.

Claudia was nineteen years old, with a story that seemed pulled straight out of a family drama. Her mother, in search of a better future, had left her behind when she was just a child, unable to take her along due to the lack of an American visa. For years, the physical and emotional distance had separated them, leaving Claudia with a void that time had not been able to fill. Now, longing to reunite with her mother, Claudia had decided to embark on this dangerous journey to the United States, despite not having seen her in nine years. The Humanitarian Parole her mother had applied for had turned into an unfulfilled promise, and Claudia decided to risk it all and cross the Darién.

Ernesto, her boyfriend, was accompanying her with the firm promise of not leaving her alone. An architect by profession, he had turned his migration experience into a personal project. With a map in hand, he marked each stop, each town, every step they took, seeking to give meaning to their wandering days. He kept a journal, a true testament to their journey, with pages full of detailed observations and sketches that captured the essence of the places they visited. For Ernesto, this journey was more than just an odyssey northward; it was a way of immortalizing each moment, giving shape and meaning to an arduous yet vibrant experience.

Claudia and Ernesto looked more like tourists than migrants. Their clothes, impeccable and carefully chosen, stood in stark contrast to the typical image of those who had crossed the Darién. Their cameras, with which they documented each stage of their journey, gave them an air of unsettling carefreeness amidst such adversity. However, speaking to them, it became clear that beneath that façade of normalcy lay a story of sacrifices and tough decisions. They were young, but they had long left their innocence behind.

Before we parted, Ernesto asked me to write my name in his journal, at the exact spot where we had met. 'I want to remember every detail,' he said with a mix of nostalgia and melancholy.

He knew that this experience, no matter how hard it was, would be something he would never live through again, and he wanted to hold on to every memory, every person who crossed his path. Documenting every-

thing, without letting the moments fade away, was his way of making sense of a journey full of uncertainty and fear.

The stage in Guatemala was particularly traumatic. Here, the law of the strongest prevailed: either you pay, or they send you back. After traveling so far, the idea of being sent back was devastating. At the checkpoints, the police, used to extorting migrants, moved with disturbing efficiency. Their fees, almost official, forced us to always have the local currency on hand; if they saw us with dollars, they took them without remorse.

The rumor that the cartels also set up checkpoints to kidnap migrants added an extra layer of anxiety. Living with the certainty that at any moment we could be captured and our families extorted for our release was a weight that sank us into despair.

To cross into Mexico, we would have to traverse a river. Although we had already survived the Darién, the fear never went away. The makeshift rafts that awaited us, made with truck tubes and precarious planks, were anything but safe. But we had no other option. Crossing into Mexico illegally was the only way to avoid being sent back. So, once again, we found ourselves putting our lives in the hands of the unknown, trusting that the river would take us to a new chapter of this endless search for a place we could finally call home.

§

Charter 9
Mexico

Mexico represents the greatest danger for immigrants on this journey. The rumors that it is the most dangerous country they will cross, and also the largest, serve as a warning that the hardship will last for several days. In Mexican territory, they run the risk of being deported or even imprisoned if they are found as irregular immigrants.

The reputation that the police in Mexico are corrupt surrounds them with fear. It is crucial to have enough cash on hand, in case they need to bribe the authorities. Additionally, this is not a journey they can complete in a single day; it will take them several days to cross, and at this point, every decision must be carefully planned. Choosing the right path is key to successfully crossing the country.

From the very first step on Mexican soil, the hostility becomes palpable, manifesting in the unfamiliar terrain, the suspicious looks, and the constant danger lurking around every corner. Migrants describe the crossing of the river from Guatemala into Mexico as a surreal experience. The murky waters that separate the two countries symbolize two completely different worlds.

Their passage through Mexico is unauthorized, and they must remain invisible. After crossing, they arrive at a small, bustling plaza, where they immediately feel the weight of living in the shadows. Any misstep could be fatal, with the constant threat of being detained by immigration agents and taken to jail.

They are advised not to travel in large groups and to blend in with the Mexicans during the various legs of the journey. Here they must separate to board the bus that will take them to Tapachula. Although the ticket is cheap, it involves significant risk. The drivers, familiar with the situation, warn about the checkpoints, making it clear that the possibility of being discovered and detained is very real.

In Tapachula, they are advised to obtain a permit, which would become the only guarantee to pass subsequent checkpoints without major problems.

Raquel:

Ana's obvious pregnancy made obtaining the permit easier. Manuel, presented as her husband, helped us avoid inquisitive glances. Although the treatment of women was slightly better than that of men, the danger remained ever-present.

The checkpoints on Mexican roads were a constant source of fear. Despite having the permit, extortion was inevitable. We always had to have money on hand, as if we had an endless supply. Every kilometer felt like we were paying tolls to hell.

The humiliating inspections served as a reminder of our vulnerability. Those without permits were taken off the bus, disappearing into the shadows of jail or unknown destinations. The three-day journey turned into a nightmare. The drivers, in whom we entrusted our lives, became merchants of our freedom. Some passengers lost all their money under the threat of the police.

In a small town called Obregón, we made the desperate decision to abandon the bus after being warned that we would be handed over to the mafia in Hermosillo. It was an act of pure survival.

Mexico presented itself as hostile territory, where danger lurked around every corner and criminal gangs kidnapped migrants for ransom. Fear became our only constant companion, and distrust, our only guide. Deportation from a migrant jail wasn't our only fear; the uncertainty about the future was even worse.

In Obregón, we found some relief from our anguish. A formal travel agency allowed us to board a bus that offered some peace of mind. During the three hours to Hermosillo, the tension slightly eased, although we remained on constant alert.

On that bus, we met Juan's family, a family also marked by the journey and the hope for a better future. Their advice and the information they shared with us were more valuable than any possession, guiding us in the next steps when we arrived in Hermosillo.

Once there, we faced the hardest decision: choosing the route to cross into the United States. Mexicali, Nogales, Juárez... three possible destinations, each with its own dangers and promises. Every minute in Mexico exposed us further, distancing us from the freedom we so longed for.

Ana:

Raquel found a virtual refuge in WhatsApp groups, where migrants like us shared vital information. These support networks became a crucial tool, almost like a survival game, where every piece of data could make the difference between moving forward or being caught.

Manuel, always cautious, suggested we stay one more night in Hermosillo. The fatigue was evident on our faces, and although exhaustion dominated us, the fear of making a bad decision was more powerful. We were running out of money, and each passing day reduced our chances of success. News of kidnappings and harassment by drug traffickers spread like a dark whisper. The situation became more serious as we moved forward.

Juan had protected his family with an almost superhuman tenacity during their journey through seven countries full of dangers. They had no one waiting for them on the other side of the border, and every step they took was a calculated risk. Thirty days of travel had left deep marks on all of us. Manuel, with his steady presence, had become our protector and anchor amid the chaos.

In Mexicali, at least we had the advantage of knowing about a shelter where we could stay, information that came from other migrants in the WhatsApp groups. However, many of us were already out of money, and decisions had to be made with cold rationality, which became more elusive with the exhaustion.

Mexico had proven to be more inhospitable than our own countries. The Mexican police made their disdain clear, and although it was said that crossing through El Paso, Texas, was easier, fear still lingered. Thousands of migrants like us were fighting for the same opportunity, but our strength was fading.

We spent two nights in Hermosillo, partly because my body no longer responded as it once did. My pregnancy had progressed, and the signs of exhaustion were undeniable. Thirty-six weeks. The birth was approaching, though I couldn't predict the exact moment. My baby, restless in my womb, seemed as eager as I was to emerge and see the world.

I feel the vibrant presence of my child, a being full of life who seems to want to conquer the world even before being born. His vigorous movements are a constant reminder of the life I am protecting within me, of the responsibility I've been given on this journey.

As we get closer to our goal, my body, shaped by motherhood, sends me unmistakable signals. The sporadic contractions and the growing pressure in my pelvis are subtle but powerful signs. My body, despite the exhaustion, continues to prepare for the miracle of birth, even as my mind pleads for more time, for just a little more patience to reach our destination.

I hide my fears and pains from Manuel and Raquel, who, always considerate, have adjusted their pace to mine. Silently, I thank them for their patience and dedication. They have become my chosen siblings, taking care of me and my baby with a tenderness that deeply moves me.

Raquel and Manuel, with unparalleled devotion, have embraced my pregnancy with a commitment that can only come from the purest love. Their sacrifice, delaying their own plans to accompany me, is a touching testament to their compassion. Every gesture of support, every word of encouragement, resonates in my heart, reminding me that I am not alone on this path.

In their company, I have found the strength of community, the power of shared love. Raquel and Manuel are more than friends; they are earthly angels who have transformed my pregnancy into a journey of hope, guiding me toward the miracle of birth with great determination.

Every decision on this journey has been a crossroads, a moment when we've had to assess the horizon and choose the path that brings us closer to our shared destination. Raquel and Manuel took on that responsibility with unwavering dedication, ensuring that each choice brought us, even just a lillle, closer to the dream we share.

With the size of my belly, jumping over a wall wasn't an option. After two days of rest in Hermosillo, we decided to take the route to Mexicali. We left the hotel at dawn. Today, for the first time in days, I felt a bit more comfortable for the journey. Juan's wife gave me a dress, and the hotel owner gave me a pair of sneakers that, though a size too big, fit my swollen feet perfectly. It was a small miracle amid so many difficulties.

I traveled with only what I had on, nothing more than the essentials. Raquel insisted that we needed to move as soon as possible. On this journey, I learned that strength doesn't lie in material things, but in the determination to keep moving forward, even when every-

thing seems to be against you. The essential part of this journey is the tenacity of spirit, the will to continue and to believe that I can write my own destiny.

We set out for Mexicali, an eight-hour journey that felt endless. We passed through several checkpoints, but to our surprise, we weren't extorted. We were so close to making it that this uneventful stretch felt like a dream, something incredible after everything we had been through.

When we arrived, we had to make an appointment to request entry into the United States. However, we still hadn't been granted one, and the people we met at the shelter told us they had been waiting for months. I didn't have that kind of time. Neither did my baby. We needed to get to the United States as soon as possible, before my body decided it was time to give birth.

We spent one night at the shelter, but the next morning we were already on our way to Tijuana. Money ceased to exist for me a long time ago, and Raquel, my guardian angel, has covered all my expenses. Her husband has sent her money several times, allowing us to keep moving forward, one step closer to our destination.

Since we left the Darién, I have been treated with more kindness by strangers than in my entire life. Unknown people have said kind words to me, touched my belly, and blessed my baby. These gestures, though small, have given me a strength I didn't know I had, reminding me that we are not alone on this journey.

We arrived in Tijuana at dawn, exhausted and hungry. The journey was longer than expected due to mechanical issues with the bus. Upon arriving at the terminal, a group of thieves surprised us; though they didn't take anything from us, Juan lost his bag, with all his valuables, including his documents. It was a hard blow, a reminder that danger still lurked at every step.

At daybreak, we tried to cross. The desperation to reach the United States had intensified to the point of becoming an urgent, almost visceral, need. As we approached the bridge, we encountered a human tide, a river of people who shared our desperation. Crossing without an appointment was impossible. The crowd, desperate, screamed and pleaded, while the tension in the air became palpable.

Manuel, normally so patient, transformed, releasing his frustration with shouts of anger. Raquel and I, filled with fear, clung to each other, trying to stay calm amid the chaos. This bridge was not the crossing we had imagined; it was a trap, a place where our hopes crashed against harsh reality.

The crowd clamored for their rights, called for help, but everything seemed futile. The bridge was blocked; no one could enter or leave. More than twelve hundred migrants were trying to cross, all speaking in Spanish, the language of despair in this case. The Venezuelan national anthem echoed in the air, a painful reminder of how far we were from home and how much we had lost.

As the day went on, the despair grew. But just when our strength was waning, a miracle happened. A cry of joy broke the silence: 'I got the appointment! I got the appointment!' We joined in the excitement, and then Raquel, with tears in her eyes, said to me, 'We got the appointment!' I could hardly believe it. We had arrived only the day before, and now we had the chance to cross.

—Tomorrow we cross, —Raquel said, and her words were a balm to our tired souls.

Those who had been waiting for months couldn't understand how we had gotten the appointment so quickly. They asked if we had paid, but we had no answer.

We only knew that, somehow, our prayers had been heard. Tomorrow we would cross.

§

Charter 10
The crossing into the United States

The United States border has become a critical and strategic point for the entry of thousands of migrants from various parts of the world. The reasons driving these people to embark on the dangerous journey to the U.S. are multiple and varied. The U.S. response to this situation has sparked an intense political and social debate, with immigration policies oscillating between more restrictive approaches, such as building walls and implementing deterrence measures, and more humanitarian stances aimed at protecting those who genuinely need it.

However, the capacity of the U.S. immigration system has been repeatedly overwhelmed, resulting in overcrowded detention centers and an asylum system under considerable pressure. Moreover, the situation at the border has implications that extend beyond the U.S., also affecting transit countries like Mexico and Central American nations, which are forced to manage the migration flow within their own territories.

In recent years, during Joe Biden's presidency, the U.S. southern border has been one of the most contentious and challenging issues. Since the beginning of his administration in January 2021, this region has experienced an unprecedented migration flow. Biden promised a more humanitarian approach to immigration, in contrast to the restrictive policies implemented by his predecessor, Donald Trump.

As part of this promise, Biden reversed several of Trump's immigration policies, including the 'Remain in Mexico' program, which forced asylum seekers to wait in Mexico while their cases were processed in the U.S. He also halted the construction of the border wall and restored, as well as expanded, asylum programs, allowing a larger number of people to apply for refuge in the U.S. This approach was seen as more open and welcoming to migrants. Additionally, he implemented more specific guidelines for deportations, prioritizing individuals with serious criminal records, rather than focusing on immigrants without a criminal background.

These policy changes have led to the perception that the U.S. border is 'open,' fueling the idea that crossing and staying in the country is now more accessible. This perception has been promoted by various factors that have influenced the growing number of people attempting to enter U.S. territory.

Ana:

The border, loaded with dreams and fears, stretched out before us. For almost four weeks, I had imagined this moment, fueled by stories from other migrants that heightened both my anxiety and my hope. At 9:00 a.m., we crossed into the United States, legally, thanks to an appointment arranged through the CBP ONE app. As I opened the app that morning, a mixture of fear and anticipation filled me. Every detail seemed crucial: the phone's battery, the internet connection, the certainty that nothing could go wrong. After so much uncertainty and difficult decisions, we were finally on U.S. soil, leaving behind a chapter of struggle and resilience.

The interview was surprisingly quick. The officer seemed more interested in processing us quickly than in delving into our reasons. The questions were few and direct, as if every wrinkle in our clothes and every hollow in our faces spoke for us. We were confirmed for entry and allowed to apply for our work permit. When I received the documents in English, I felt a mix of relief and confusion. I knew those papers were our ticket in, our legitimization, even though I didn't fully understand their contents. Despite the confusion, joy prevailed: we had made it.

Crossing the border was overwhelming. From Mexico, the U.S. side already seemed like a different world, but experiencing it was something else. The offices were modern, spotless, designed to reflect the efficiency and order of this new country. The white walls, gleaming furniture, and signs in English all reminded us that we were in a different place, where the rules were different. My pregnancy, though obvious, seemed to go unnoticed amid the bureaucracy; they only asked if I needed medical attention. I lied and said no, fearing that admitting otherwise might jeopardize our entry.

The hours of waiting dragged on, each minute presenting a new challenge for my exhausted body. We watched the officials move in perfect sync, playing their part in the border machinery. Finally, around 2:00 p.m., we got the signal. We were ready to enter. I felt such immense relief that I almost collapsed. The border was behind us, and before us unfolded a new landscape, where everything seemed brighter, more orderly. I looked around, searching for some sign that this was real, that I wasn't dreaming. The very air seemed different, lighter, full of promise.

Unconsciously, I stroked my belly and whispered, 'My son, we've begun our American dream.' That phrase, more than a promise, was an affirmation that all the sacrifice had been worth it. For a long time, I had wondered if this moment would come, if we would manage to cross and find our place in this vast country. And now, here we were, with a future ahead of us.

Raquel's husband was waiting for us in San Diego, which shortened our journey. We gave the address where he was staying so that the papers could be sent there. They told us the residency would take about six months to arrive, but that seemed like a minor detail compared to what we had achieved. Although we were only an hour away from our final destination, that last leg of the trip felt endless. The accumulated fatigue was starting to take its toll, and my body, which had endured every test until then, began to rebel. The pain in my belly reminded me of how exhausted I was.

The truth is, at that moment, I didn't care about what I was hearing; I just needed to arrive and rest. Finally, I felt that the journey was over. That night, exhausted, I told Raquel that I couldn't walk any further. My voice, usually firm, was barely a whisper. She, concerned, insisted that I should see a doctor. But my fear was greater; I was afraid that any complication would send us back to the starting point. I stayed in bed for two days, *feeling the weight of the pregnancy. Every part of my body hurt so much that I felt completely broken.*

Every movement was a monumental effort, and my swollen feet barely supported me. I couldn't even put on my shoes, and just looking at them made me think about everything I had left behind. The exhaustion was overwhelming, as if every cell in my body was protesting against the effort it had taken to get here.

On the second day in the United States, the contractions began, each one more intense than the last. Sweat poured down my forehead as panic set in. Raquel, with an urgency I hadn't seen before, rushed me to a nearby hospital. It was clear that I was in labor. I felt each contraction like a wave pulling me under, clinging to the idea that soon I would have my son in my arms.

Each contraction tore through me and made me feel like I couldn't hold on, I couldn't breathe, the pain was unbearable. When we arrived, a medical team greeted me with efficiency and warmth. More than fifteen people moved around me, each with a specific task, making sure everything was fine. I didn't understand what they were saying, as they all spoke in English, but I knew they were concerned about me. I had never seen anything like it in my life: I was in a room that felt almost like five stars; they gave me socks and underwear, I didn't lack for anything.

In my country, Venezuela, hospitals were small, and we never had this many resources or medical staff. I had never been in a delivery room, but based on what I had heard, no one had told me anything like this. My mother, on the other hand, told me that when my siblings and I were born, she practically had to give birth on the floor, in the middle of nowhere, enduring the pain until a doctor was available to attend to her.

Here, I was surrounded by a level of care I never imagined possible, providing me with everything I needed for my well-being. I felt that, for the first time in a long while, I was in a safe place. After eighteen hours of intense labor, on April 30, 2023, my son came into the world at Sharp Coronado Hospital.

When I held him for the first time, after pain that tore me apart inside, I felt my heart explode with love. My son, a robust boy weighing 3,950 kg and measuring 54 cm, had been born on American soil. I held him, in disbelief, and amidst tears, I showered him with kisses. We made it, my son, we made it.

A few hours after his birth, someone from the government visited me, or at least I think so, and they asked me what his name would be. The woman didn't speak Spanish and, with a translator, she asked me questions. I will name him Diego. Before, my baby didn't have a name, and I decided to call him that in honor of the city that welcomed us.

In that moment, I realized that every step taken, every sacrifice, had been rewarded. My son was born in the United States, just as I had always dreamed. Had I been delayed any longer, Diego would have been born in Mexico, but now, against all odds, we had succeeded. And as I gazed at his small face, I knew that everything had been worth it.

This chapter of our lives began with uncertainty, but now, holding my son in my arms, I knew we were destined for something great. Every sacrifice, every tear shed along the way, had been for him, for this moment, for the promise of a better life in this new land. And although the road ahead was still uncertain, I was ready to face it, with Diego by my side, in this new home that already began to feel like ours.

§

Charter 11
The American Dream

The American dream, for undocumented immigrants who cross the border, is nothing more than a mirage that disguises a ruthless and discouraging reality. It's a truth that hits them mercilessly, like a cold wind in the night, revealing how little they knew about the world they were entering.

The apparent happiness they feel upon setting foot on U.S. soil fades as they begin to understand the system. The documents they receive are nothing more than a court date with an immigration judge to face a deportation process. What they show on social media is just a distorted reflection of what really awaits them; a facade that hides the abyss of uncertainty and despair that many fall into.

Immigrants venture into a country whose language they do not know, completely unaware of the reality and trapped in a legal maze with no way out. Not knowing where to start is the first problem. The promise of a better life dissolves in the face of the constant threat of deportation.

To dispel their doubts, they need to make appointments with professionals who speak their language, who can clearly explain what is happening, what the real meaning is of being subjected to a deportation process, and whether they will actually be deported. When they finally understand the reality, it seems illogical to them how they managed to cross the border and what those documents, which contradict what they initially believed, really mean.

They are informed about the possibility of presenting an asylum application before the judge in order to obtain a work permit while a final decision is made. However, what they do not know is that receiving asylum approval requires meeting very specific criteria.

The protection they need is often far removed from the eligibility criteria for asylum. The law requires specific reasons to grant this benefit and allow them to remain in the United States, and the experiences of many immigrants do not align with those requirements.

They arrive in the country stripped of any material possessions, and their dreams do not translate into fortune. Despite this, they are required to hire a licensed attorney to defend their cases, with fees ranging from five to twelve thousand dollars.

How can someone who just arrived and has no work permit be expected to cover these fees? Their language barrier prevents them from navigating the legal paths on their own, and their uncertain situation makes them easy prey for scams.

Raising the necessary money to start their legal processes becomes a race against time, as the asylum application must be submitted within the first year of their arrival. Their immigration status leaves them unsteady: they cannot find decent jobs because they don't have a work permit, but working illegally can have serious consequences for obtaining immigration benefits in the future.

Paying for legal assistance does not guarantee success in their process, as there is no magic formula for achieving regularization through this means. There is no guaranteed happy ending, and the permanent residency that many believe will arrive magically in six months is an illusion. For many, winning an asylum case is nearly impossible, especially when their reasons do not align with the categories established by the law.

Immigrants try to follow the process, submit an application, and wait for the judge's final decision. However, the conviction that they can move the judge with their stories, which do not meet the eligibility criteria, fades with the final decision.

For the United States, it is also a limitation to have so many immigrants in its territory who do not speak the language. In today's news, we see officers detaining immigrants without being able to understand what they are trying to say.

After facing reality and trying to understand how Ana could achieve legal status, she found herself trapped in an abyss, fearing she would lose everything. After hiring a lawyer and paying more than six thousand dollars for assistance, she was simply told what she already suspected: she is not eligible for asylum in the United States. Everything she has lived through in her life does not fit the U.S. law's criteria for granting this benefit and preventing her deportation. However, filled with emotion, she decides to tell the truth at her hearing.

Ana, during her hearing, explains to the judge:

Honorable Judge, first I want to thank you for listening to me at this moment, and apologize for having crossed the border of your country, which is the reason I am here before you.

I am an abused woman; since my childhood, I have been mistreated. I was abused in the streets when I was young and was just a vendor selling goods to help my siblings. Throughout my life, I have suffered various forms of mistreatment from people, from the police, and from anyone who wanted to, because no one defended me. I grew up with every possible deprivation. My reasons for fleeing Venezuela are based on the abuse I received from my partner, and I have no evidence either, it's all in my mind.

In my case, Andrés, my abuser, no longer pursues me—he stayed in Venezuela—but it's a reality that I know he must be angry because I left him. If I were to return, he might look for me and beat me.

The persecution continues in my life. My ex-partner is still an enemy, and I know exactly what he is capable of. Additionally, I no longer have anywhere to go; I have no home. Poverty haunts me, as does the lack of opportunities, like a constant shadow that follows me from my past and is also my present reality. Here, in this country, I've managed to sustain myself 100%, even though I live in a rented house. It's a place I can afford with the work I do.

I am in this final hearing fully aware that I will not be granted asylum; that's what my lawyer, who has much experience in these types of cases, has told me. So, what did I pay for? Why did I make the effort to seek assistance?

How can I convey to you the constant fear I feel of falling back into misery? How can I make you understand that it's not just the physical danger that terrifies me, but the return to a life without hope, where each day is a struggle just to survive?

My childhood was a mosaic of deprivation. Every day was a battle to get through the previous one. The taunts from my classmates were wounds that never fully healed. The lack of resources marked us deeply, turning each Christmas without gifts into a reminder of our poverty. The nights without electricity or water were silent witnesses to our desperation; sometimes, we simply couldn't afford the utilities, and the little *food we had at home would spoil, leaving my siblings and me without food.*

In that environment, I learned to fear the future, to expect nothing more than a continuous struggle to stay afloat. Today, that same struggle has shifted to a different stage, but it's no less terrifying. As I try to defend my asylum case, the constant fear of being deported consumes me. The prospect of returning to a country where poverty and the lack of opportunities await me and my son Diego is a living nightmare.

I don't want to see Diego grow up in a place where food is rationed, where medical care is an unattainable luxury. This thought haunts me every day. I have spent months without sleep, thinking about this moment, about what you will say to me, about what I should really tell you.

Diego, my son, is an American citizen. I did everything I could to ensure he was born here, and now he is protected by this country's laws. The idea that he could be taken from my side because I do not deserve asylum in this nation is unbearable to me. I don't know if that's true or just a rumor, but it haunts me in every thought.

Is it fair that a child, born in this land of opportunity, be expelled alongside his mother? Or, worse yet, be separated from her, destined to grow up in a foster family, far from a mother's love and warmth? This thought suffocates me, fills me with a desperation that only a mother can understand.

Our struggle as immigrants goes far beyond the courts and immigration hearings. It's a battle for survival, for the opportunity to offer our children a better life than the one we had. It's a war against injustice, against a system that seems designed to break us. And although the American dream is often elusive, the fight for a dignified and safe life never stops.

At the end of the day, what I'm pursuing is not just a document that allows me to stay in this country. It's the chance to ensure that my son Diego has a bright future, a future where he doesn't have to know the miseries I experienced. That is the real reason I keep fighting day after day, even when everything seems to be against me. Because for him, for his well-being, the sacrifice is always worth it, and the American dream, though out of reach, remains the light that guides my way.

When I arrived in the United States, I didn't come seeking comfort or intending to take advantage of the system. I came with a simple and honest dream: to build a better future for myself and my son, a future that had become unattainable in my homeland, Venezuela. However, what I found after crossing the border was a reality far harsher and more discouraging than I could have ever imagined.

The reason that drove me to leave my country wasn't just the economic misery, but something much more personal and painful: the abuse from my partner, Andrés. Leaving Venezuela wasn't a decision I made lightly; it was an act of desperation, an extreme measure to escape from a situation that had become unbearable. Andrés wasn't just physically violent, he had turned my life into a hell of emotional and psychological abuse. With every hurtful word, with every whispered threat in the dark, he dismantled my self-esteem until I found myself trapped in an invisible cage, built from fear and manipulation.

From the moment I woke up to the moment I fell asleep, I lived under the shadow of his abuse. The terror of what might trigger his anger became my constant companion. I knew that any word or gesture could be the spark that ignited his fury. But what terrified me the most was his capacity for unpredictable violence, which could erupt out of nowhere, like an unexpected storm, leaving only destruction in its wake.

It wasn't just my life that was in danger, but also my son's, who hadn't yet been born but was already exposed to that toxic environment. The thought that my son might grow up surrounded by violence, that his first memories might be of shouting, of fear, of doors slamming, filled me with indescribable despair. I couldn't allow his life to begin in such a home, where safety was an unreachable luxury and love, an empty word.

Finally, I made the decision to flee. I did it not just for myself, but for my son, for the life I carried within me that deserved something better. I left everything behind, hoping to find refuge in the United States, a place where the torment of my past couldn't reach us, where I could start over. I didn't know what awaited me on the other side of the border, but I knew that anything would be better than the hell I was escaping.

The United States represented more than just a place on the map for me; it was the promise of a new life, one in which fear no longer dictated my every decision. I came seeking safety and protection, hoping to build a home where my son could grow up without knowing the cruelty I had endured. Although the path ahead of me was full of obstacles, I was determined to fight for that second chance, for that dream that, though difficult, could still become a reality.

Your Honor, I stand before you with the truth laid bare and my heart in my hands. I did not cross that border to violate your laws or to take advantage of the system you hold dear. I swear to you, Your Honor, that this was never my intention. I came here for a much deeper, more human, more desperate reason. I crossed that border because I had no other choice. After traveling through all of Latin America, I realized that there is no safe place for anyone, that systems worsen the further north we go. The closer we get to the United States, the greater the corruption, and the more dangerous the streets become. Fleeing my country was my only way out because my son's life and mine were in danger. His father does not want us, and there is a ruling power that keeps us away from any opportunity.

What mother wouldn't do the same? What mother wouldn't give everything to protect her child?

In Venezuela, my life had become a living hell. Violence wasn't an occasional event; it was a constant shadow. In the neighborhood where I lived, people were murdered for something as simple as a cellphone. No matter how hard we worked, we were always drowning in poverty. Speaking out against the government was impossible, and those who did were punished. I lived in fear, Your Honor, fear of everything, fear of continuing to live.

I know that my reasons for seeking asylum do not perfectly align with the laws written in this country. But I ask you to look beyond the words in the law books and see the reality of my situation. I'm not asking for privileges. I'm not asking for more than what any human being deserves: the chance to live without fear, to give my son a future where he can grow up without the constant fear of violence, hunger, and lack of opportunity.

Your Honor, I only crossed the border in search of safety. I made an appointment, I complied with the requirements your country imposed on me, and my entry was authorized. My only crime is being poor, like many others in this room. Or do you see many wealthy people passing through here? I don't think so. The rich aren't in deportation proceedings because they don't need to cross borders or go unnoticed; the world always opens doors for them.

Your Honor, I beg you to put yourself in my shoes, if only for a moment. Imagine that I were your daughter, that Diego were your grandson. Wouldn't you do everything possible to protect us? Wouldn't you move heaven and earth to make sure we were safe?

That's all I'm asking for: the chance to give my son a dignified life, a life not marked by fear and desperation.

I have nothing more to say. If my fate is deportation, so be it. But before you make your decision, I wanted to make sure you knew the whole truth. Because I know that in this country, the truth is valued. My story is not just mine; it's the story of thousands of mothers, fathers, and children fleeing the same nightmare. And if I ask for anything, Your Honor, it's that you allow me to take my son with me. Diego is all I have, and the only thing I want is to protect him, to give him the life I always dreamed of for him, even if that dream is fleeting.

Reflection:

The silence in the courtroom is deafening. The lawyer, astonished by the account, watches the prosecutor's reaction. Every word of Ana's resonates in the minds of those who hear her, connecting her suffering with that of millions of migrants who have fled in search of a spark of hope in a world that too often closes its doors to them. Those present are surprised to hear this woman's perspective, to see how many opportunities she perceives in this land.

The judge, faced with such testimony, cannot help but question the balance between law and compassion.

What weight will this testimony have in his decision? That is left to the imagination of each reader, in the balance of their own judgment.

We leave the decision in his hands, knowing that their lives hang by a thread. And as they wait, they can only ask themselves: if you were the judge, what decision would you have made?

§

Charter 12
Human Trafficking

The United States has demonstrated a firm commitment to the fight against human trafficking, also known as trafficking in persons. This crime, which exploits individuals for forced labor or sexual exploitation, constitutes a grave violation of human rights. Both nationally and internationally, the U.S. government has implemented various policies and programs to combat this atrocious crime. In collaboration with foreign governments, non-governmental organizations (NGOs), and international agencies, it has focused its efforts on eradicating human trafficking, particularly in the border regions with Mexico. Additionally, the U.S. supports the countries of the Northern Triangle of Central America, such as Guatemala, Honduras, and El Salvador. The United States funds programs aimed at preventing this scourge by strengthening judicial institutions, protecting human rights, and improving economic conditions, with the goal of reducing people's vulnerability to exploitation.

However, the reality in the Darién jungle highlights a grim contradiction to this commitment. This inhospitable migratory route, one of the most dangerous in the world, is used by thousands of migrants in their attempt to reach the American dream. In this region, migrants are subjected to extreme vulnerability, exploited mercilessly by human traffickers, known locally as 'coyotes' or 'polleros.' These criminals promise to guide migrants through the jungle in exchange for large sums of money; however, many of them subject their victims to physical, sexual, and economic abuse. Women and children are particularly vulnerable to sexual violence and exploitation on this cruel journey.

Abuse by traffickers has a devastating impact on victims, extending far beyond physical suffering. Human trafficking in the Darién not only poses a deadly risk due to extreme conditions and violence, but it also leaves deep psychological and emotional scars. Migrants subjected to exploitation and abuse often face severe trauma, such as post-traumatic stress disorder (PTSD), anxiety, and depression. Experiences of sexual abuse and physical violence have long-lasting effects, impacting both the mental and emotional health of the victims, making it difficult for them to rebuild their lives.

The situation is further exacerbated by fear and distrust of authorities, combined with a lack of access to adequate justice systems. The transnational nature of this route makes law enforcement a monumental challenge, resulting in many crimes going unpunished. International organizations, such as the UN and the Red Cross, have raised alarms about the severity of the situation in the Darién and have provided humanitarian aid, including shelter, food, and psychological support to migrants who manage to traverse the jungle. However, available resources are limited, while the needs of the migrants are immense.

The figure of the guide in the Darién has become a symbol of both desperation and exploitation. Although their role is crucial for migration through one of the most inhospitable regions of the Americas, their activity is marked by illegality and abuse. The guides, who should initially be intermediaries of hope, often turn into ruthless exploiters, taking advantage of the migrants' desperation to enrich themselves at the expense of their suffering.

In Colombia, this activity has reached almost industrial dimensions. The fees for crossing from Necoclí to Capurganá vary depending on nationality, with Venezuelans paying more than Colombians. The journey, far from being one of hope, becomes a harrowing experience in which migrants are reduced to mere numbers. Those without money suffer delays and are often forced to work under precarious conditions to cover their expenses. Planning the journey involves difficult decisions, such as what provisions to carry and how to balance the weight of each item, while each step becomes a physical and emotional challenge.

The psychological impact of human trafficking is devastating. Migrants who suffer abuse often experience a sense of desolation and hopelessness that can persist long after they have reached their destination.

The lack of access to psychological support and adequate healthcare services further worsens the situation of migrants, leaving them in a state of extreme vulnerability. While the number of people who have managed to cross the Darién is alarming, it is even more disturbing to consider the number of those who have not made it.

A true gesture of defending human rights is to recognize that what is happening in the Darién jungle cannot be ignored. The current situation exposes a network of exploitation that feeds on the dreams and desperation of those seeking a better life. The sale of empty promises and the economic exploitation of those fleeing their lands has turned this journey into one of suffering and abuse. The migration from Colombia to the United States comes at a much higher cost than a simple first-class flight; for migrants, it costs them their dignity, their safety, and in many cases, their lives.

It is imperative to demand a stronger and more humane response from those responsible for regulating this situation. Immigration policies must address the root of the problem from a human rights perspective, and international efforts must be intensified to protect migrants at every stage of their journey. Only in this way can the shadow that darkens the American dream be mitigated, and every human being be guaranteed the dignity and respect they deserve. It is a moral duty and an urgent necessity to ensure that the hope for a better life does not become a pretext for a new form of slavery in the Darién jungle.

Understanding why migrants continue to choose the north as their final destination, after having crossed all of Central America, calls for an analysis of the policies and internal structures of each country. The references to their journey are deeply concerning, especially during their passage through Mexico. While the aim is not to pursue a policy that openly facilitates migration, it is essential that the governments involved work together to balance the region.

The situation that has affected Venezuela in recent years, along with the silence of neighboring nations, has been the main reason why Venezuelans have decided to leave their country. Tired of the internal situation, more than seven million

Venezuelans have dispersed around the world. Currently, the country is experiencing one of the most blatant electoral frauds of the technological era, where the will expressed by machines is contradicted by human decisions.

Since 2022, Venezuelan migration has been primarily composed of less privileged individuals who only aspire to the security of being able to feed themselves. Willing to do hard labor, many of them have joined the workforce in the United States.

In 2024, outdated legislation should no longer be applied, as it does not reflect the current reality. Laws no longer instill the same fear in people, especially given the language barrier they face when emigrating to the United States.

As human beings, we must unite to protect migrants from the unnecessary dangers they face today.

§

General Production

Solanyely Ruiz

September 2024

Editorial Production

www.oediciones.com

September 2024

This editorial piece is an expression of
premium quality and academic integrity, where
a series of knowledge is combined, from the
creation of its content to the finishing touches
in each stage of production.

www.oediciones.com